DEAD RECKONINGS

A Review of Horror and the Weird in the Arts
Edited by Alex Houstoun and Michael J. Abolafia

No. 23 (Spring 2018)

DEAD RECKONINGS is published by Hippocampus Press, P.O. Box 641, New York, NY 10156 (www.hippocampuspress.com). Copyright © 2018 by Hippocampus Press. Cover art by Jason C. Eckhardt. Cover design by Barbara Briggs Silbert. Hippocampus Press logo by Anastasia Damianakos. Orders and subscriptions should be sent to Hippocampus Press. Contact Alex Houstoun at deadreckoningsjournal@gmail.com for assignments or before submitting a publication for review.

ISSN 1935-6110
ISBN 978-1-61498-224-1

Introduction to Japanese Vampire Fiction

Darrell Schweitzer

KAZUKI SAKURABA. *A Small Charred Face*. Translated by Jocelyne Allen. San Francisco: Haiku Soru, 2017. 240 pp. $15.99 tpb. ISBN: 978-1-4215-9541-2.

I don't claim to have a deep knowledge of East Asian fantasy fiction; better than nothing, in that I have even written introductions to volumes of Japanese Cthulhu Mythos fiction, but still my knowledge is superficial. Sure, there are the "Oriental tales" written by Westerners over the past couple of centuries, but they're not the same thing. Hopefully some of us have read Lafcadio Hearn, or *Strange Stories from a Chinese Studio* and the like, but what about the moderns? Contemporaries? Contemporary Japanese YA vampire fiction? Some of my comments might seem naïve to a Japanese reader, but all I can say is that Ms. Sakuraba's novel (which might be classifiable as a young adult book, or even as a romance) seems a good place to start. If a territory is unknown, the best thing to do is start exploring.

We are here presented was a completely novel form of the vampire, called a Bamboo, allegedly because such creatures originated in China and were the spirits of the bamboo forests, where an unwary child could easily disappear. A colony of them has moved to Japan and blended in with the population. The Bamboo drink blood, of humans or animals, but they are not reanimated corpses or hungry ghosts. They are living beings with strange powers (including the ability to fly) who live for about 120 years, then disintegrate into a cloud of white blossoms and are gone. Like Western vampires, they are allergic to sunlight. Unlike Western vampires, they are moral creatures, not necessarily evil at all, and governed by their own strict laws, the foremost of which is that they must not make contact with humans or reveal their secrets to the humans they live among. But Bamboo are also capable of love and of forming forbidden attachments to humans, and therein lies the tale. It is possible for a human to become a Bamboo, if a Bamboo drinks some, but not all, of the blood of a living person. To avoid such complications, law-abiding Bamboo prefer fresh corpses.

In the first and longest segment of the book, we meet Ryo, a boy whose gangster stepfather has so offended the local mafia that the entire family is massacred. Ryo hides and meets a Bamboo, who was politely waiting outside the house for the victims to die, so he could come in and drink their blood. Instead of leaving Ryo to be murdered (the assassins are waiting downstairs, knowing one boy is missing), the Bamboo rescues him, and Ryo grows up raised by two affectionate substitute-fathers, both Bamboo. But since the mafia is still looking for a boy, the Bamboo disguise Ryo as a girl, and so he grows up, ages ten to about eighteen, as a girl. Meanwhile the two Bamboo have gotten in trouble with the Bamboo authorities and one has been put to death. Ryo (still as a girl) made friends with a rogue Bamboo girl who looks like a teenager but is actually very old, nearing the end of her lifespan. The two of them roam about, having adventures, while the Bamboo girl, Marika, actually kills people on occasion. Marika, whose carelessness caused all the trouble, ends up buried alive for some years, but survives, minus an arm. Ryo, resuming life as a man, has a haunted existence. He meets one of his Bamboo friends toward the end of their lives.

In the second section Marika goes on, having befriended and partnered with another human child, but she is never as successful or as compassionate as Yoji and Mustah, who raised Ryo.

In the final section we learn how the Bamboo were driven out of China, and the origin of their own rigid regime. This sequence seems to take place well before the rest of the novel. We see one character in it (the poetry reading Bamboo) who might by Yoji, well before he met Ryo.

What is good about this book, other than its sheer originality (at least for Western readers), is its characters, who are quite real and vivid. I find two weaknesses, or at least bothersome points. The narrative is very much aware of sexuality, but we never quite have a sense of how Ryo's experiences have shaped his own sexual identity. The matter even presses the limits of credibility, since by seventeen or eighteen most boys have had a voice change and begun to sprout facial hair and would have a much harder time

impersonating a girl than at age ten. Yoji and Mustah might be seen as a very successful gay couple, but we are not exactly sure how Ryo feels about sexual identity. Then there is the matter of chronology. The novel seems to take place in an endless modernity, a word of automobiles and telephones and the like. Yet Ryo actually grows old. Marika is more than a hundred by the time the story is done. Does this mean that the action started back around 1910 or so, or that it extends into the future, to 2050 at the earliest? There is no sense of this. In the final section, we learn that the Bamboo were driven out of China during the Cultural Revolution, i.e., circa 1970, which would seem to push the action well into our own future. The author does not seem to have given much thought to the timeline of the action.

The translation reads well, idiomatic without slipping too far into slanginess. The story keeps moving, often in unconventional ways, and sometimes reveals surprising depths of feeling. Some passages are very moving. This is a book well worth a look.

The Coming Singer: Early Critical Responses to Clark Ashton Smith

Scott Connors

George Sterling's sonnet "The Coming Singer" has been described by one critic as an expression "of his hope for a new major poetic voice."[1] Unknown to contemporary readers (and apparently to that critic), Sterling's poem was inspired by his protégé, the young bard of the Sierra foothills Clark Ashton Smith. Although Sterling made it abundantly clear in correspondence that the poem was dedicated to Smith, his memories of the controversy surrounding Ambrose Bierce and his championship of Sterling's poem "A Wine of Wizardry" persuaded him that his advocacy of the younger poet's work must not appear to smack of anything suggesting cronyism or, as he called it, "log rolling." It was because of this experience that Sterling vetoed both Smith's suggested dedication of his first collection, *The Star-Treader and Other Poems* (A. M. Robertson, 1912), and the dedicatory poem (beginning "High priest of this our later Song," unpublished until after Smith's death) with which Smith wished to open the collection.

Sterling apparently saw his role as that of a poetic John the Baptist, or to use a metaphor more in keeping with weird fiction, he was to be the opener of the way for Smith into the wider literary world. He mentioned this in a magazine interview, wherein he expressed both his indebtedness to Bierce and his sincere admiration for Smith's work: "This boy [Smith] has a wonderful gift, if I know anything about such things."[2] Sterling concluded the interview by quoting in full Smith's sonnet "The Last Night." When Boutwell Dunlap, one of Smith's acquaintances from Auburn,

---

1. Thomas E. Benediktsson, *George Sterling* (Boston: Twayne, 1980), 115. "The Coming Singer" was first published (without dedication) in Sterling's *Beyond the Breakers and Other Poems* (1914). It was also included in *Sonnets to Craig*, a cycle of poems dedicated to Upton Sinclair's future wife Mary Craig Sinclair (1928).

2. Edward F. O'Day, "Varied Types XVII—George Sterling," *Town Talk* (15 April 1911): 8.

brought the boy to San Francisco and introduced him to the press, Sterling was on hand to supply pithy and pertinent comments regarding Smith's precocious genius. These were to appear as part of a campaign to boost sales of Smith's book when it finally appeared. However, delays and a comedy of errors caused premature appearance of the publicity articles in early August 1912.[3]

It is not surprising, considering their genesis as part of a press junket (which included handing out of copies of some of Smith's poems as well as publicity photographs of the young singer), that the newspaper articles, which appeared in all the major San Francisco dailies, share certain similarities. They all quote extensively from Smith's poem "Nero," the *Bulletin* and the *San Francisco Evening Post* doing so in its entirety. Being news articles rather than critical reviews, the stories are light on analysis but heavy on quoting from "local men of sound literary judgment and competent critical ability."[4] Rather than discuss the poems on their own merits, the reporters instead record the opinions of the local Solons who have seen the poems. This elicited comparisons of Smith to many other poets, some appropriate (Keats and Byron), others not (Dryden and Pope), but in each case without the comparison being explained or substantiated. Likewise, all the newspapers made much of Smith's isolated rural background and youth. Smith's limited education[5] was much discussed, in continuance of a tradition of "'natural' and 'artless'" poets whose genius "had been happily protected by social barriers from the refinements of civilization and advanced literary art."[6]

Two of the news articles, in the *Bulletin* (August 5, 1912) and the *Evening Post* (August 10, 1912), stand out from the rest. The *Bulletin*'s headline, "Genius Flashes from the Sierras. Auburn Boy

---

3. See Scott Connors, "Who Discovered Clark Ashton Smith?" *Lost Worlds: The Journal of Clark Ashton Smith Studies* No. 1 (2003): 25–34.

4. "California Youth Is Hailed by Critics as Poetical Genius. George [sic] Ashton Smith, Aged 19, Writes Poems Pronounced by Literati as Ranking with Best of Keats and Byron," *San Francisco Chronicle* (2 August 1912): 6.

5. Although Smith was admitted to the Placer Union High School, his shyness, shame over his poverty, and conviction that he could provide himself a better education led him to withdraw after only a few days.

6. M. H. Abrams, *The Mirror and the Lamp* (1953; rpt. London: Oxford University Press, 1971), 83.

is Called Keats' Equal. Wealth of Language and Beauty of Imagery Amaze the Critics," starts off in much the same manner as other articles, but then the writer constructs an original argument that concludes with a cogent appraisal of "Nero" and how it differs from others of Smith's poems:

> Clark Ashton Smith, the 19-year-old boy poet of Auburn, Cal., whom both George Sterling and Ambrose Bierce declare to be the author of poems in no way inferior to those of Keats, offers a strange example of genius purely original. This boy, who writes of stars and planets and towering ambitions with the force and brilliance of an inspired poet, was born near the Sierra foothill town, and until a few months ago never went further from Auburn than a day's walk. [. . .]
>
> Smith is self-educated, having attended the Placer High School but a short time. He is of a lonely, dreamy disposition, not easily making acquaintances, and generally preferring his own society to that of other people. He is an omnivorous reader and has long found the Auburn library too narrow for his desires.
>
> Without ever hearing good music, Smith has written an "Ode to Music" of a strangely idealistic tone; for the most part, however, his imagination loves to scale the firmament and soar among the stars and measureless abysses where, as he writes, "Crouching Silence, thunder potent, sleeps."
>
> His poem, "Nero," published herewith, is considered his finest. It shows what none of his other poems shows, perception of a human motive[,] for this boy's dominant note is a rapt remoteness from earthly things.[7]

Sophie Treadwell, later a distinguished thespian and playwright, had no fear of being "scooped," since her assessment of Clark did not appear until August 10, 1912, in her regular book review column in the *Evening Post*. This additional time allowed her to

---

7. "Genius Flashes From the Sierras. Auburn Boy Is Called Keats' Equal. C. Ashton Smith, Aged Nineteen, Hailed As Poet. Wealth of Language and Beauty of Imagery Among the Critics," [San Francisco] *Bulletin* (5 August 1912): 5. The unsigned author of this laudatory article was Ernest Jerome Hopkins, later a distinguished scholar of Ambrose Bierce, and an acquaintance of Smith's from when he was a schoolteacher in Auburn. See Clark Ashton Smith, letter to George Sterling, 8 August 1912, *The Shadow of the Unattained: The Letters of George Sterling and Clark Ashton Smith*, ed. David E. Schultz and S. T. Joshi (New York: Hippocampus Press, 2005), 55 (hereafter *SU*).

synthesize the best coverage and to contemplate Smith's poetry without the pressures of a deadline. While quoting the same Sterling statement as did Hopkins, Treadwell offers this assessment of the significance of his support of the new poet: "Poetry is finding its kingdom in the empire of the West. A boy of nineteen comes down from the Sierras and George Sterling is waiting to hand over to him the laurel wreath the same that Ambrose Bierce handed over to him."[8] She correctly identifies the predominant mood of Smith's work as that of "remoteness, aloofness from earthly affairs" and states that "Nero" is an exception to this. However, as Porter Garnett would note later, the poem represents the infusion of earthly themes with cosmic significance rather than an embrace of the purely mundane.

Unfortunately, this publicity arrived three months too soon, and Ambrose Bierce expressed concern that the "lions of reaction" would descend upon the young Clark Ashton Smith.[9] Bierce's fears were not unfounded. The poet Witter Bynner took a few verbal potshots at Smith and Sterling, referring to them in a magazine interview as "the Star Dust Twins."[10] *Current Literature* stated that "a reading of the poems in question, while it reveals a genuine talent and a mastery of words remarkable in so young a writer, fails to justify the superlative praise which has come from some of the California newspapers."[11]

When Aleck Robertson finally published *The Star-Treader* in November 1912, the tone of the articles was much different from that of the previous summer. This was to be expected to some extent, since coverage was now in the hands of experienced book reviewers who had more than a few poems upon which to base their judgment. Sophie Treadwell's review in the November 23, 1912 issue of the *San Francisco Evening Post* is easily the most negative review that *The Star-Treader* received:

---

8. Sophie Treadwell, "Makers of Books and Some Recent Works," *San Francisco Post* (10 August 1912): 6.

9. Ambrose Bierce, "Letter from Ambrose Bierce," *Town Talk* (10 August 1912): 11. In *A Much Misunderstood Man: Selected Letters of Ambrose Bierce*, ed. S. T. Joshi and David E. Schultz (Columbus: Ohio State University Press, 2003), 225.

10. O'Day, "Varied Types XC—Witter Bynner," *Town Talk* (7 September 1912): 7.

11. "Recent Poetry," *Current Literature* 53, No. 5 (October 1912): 473.

Clark Ashton Smith's little book of poems has proved a hard disappointment to me. I had heard so much, read so much of this young genius of the Sierras, this new-discovered greater-than-Keats, that I ventured into the promising-looking book with awed expectancy. For me, there is little, nothing near to Keats. But there is something near to Sterling; the lesser part of Sterling.

Stars, suns, comets, abysses, moon, have been the strongest inspirers of the boy; and it is where he plunges into these vastnesses and voids that he is lost. [. . .]

Within a page and a half of this poem appear the words unhorizoned, undimensioned. unborn, unswerved, unconstrainable, undiscoverable, unstriving; and later, ungrasped, unsure, unfound, unexceeded.

The diction throughout is unusual. The lad shows a fondness for the more weighty forms of expression—what might be called "near Latin." He has a strong penchant for obsolete words, and words which apparently are of home brew. Consider that expression, "frory beamlessness." Is that not delightfully reminiscent of Lewis Carroll, and "unescapable alternity, mystic immanence, cadences of threne, pits of infinite duress, mazeful gyres, star-undominated gyres, unswervable eclipse, gyre-release, unsphered restorelessly, murkiness, levins, cerementless, immingle, conterminate, malefice, clomb, discorporate," and many, many more. When these tread fast and furious one upon the other, the exhausted reader can but wonder why the publishers did not warn with a more definite title. Why not "The Unrevealed," or "The Mystic Meaning," or perhaps "The Shadow of Nightmare"?[12]

Treadwell concludes with an exquisite parody of Smith, beginning "Out from its incunabula my spirit burst / And wild-eyed flung its body-bonds aside . . .," and concluding "For as aloft I swung / Borei-eyed, drenched with gloom / I heard soft cheering words / That throbbed fair semitones and wizard sounds / Reverberating on from orb to orb / And waking kindred echoes in my soul— / Sweet to me as my own words sterling ring." (This last line is of course a pun on George Sterling's advocacy of Smith's work.)

Treadwell's review encapsulates the basic points which critics

12. Sophie Treadwell, "Makes of Books and Some Recent Works." *San Francisco Evening Post* (23 November 1912). In "Contemporary Reviews of Clark Ashton Smith," *The Freedom of Fantastic Things*, ed. Scott Connors (New York: Hippocampus Press, 2006), 43–5 (hereafter *FFT*).

would make against the young Clark Ashton Smith.

- *His work was too heavily influenced by that of George Sterling and others*

> A very impressionable young man is Clark Ashton Smith, taking the swift impress of Nature the more readily if she hap to be in her moods of mystery. Taking also the swift impress of other poets. It may be the Tennyson of "In Memoriam," it may be the Browning of "Childe Roland;" but principally it is Keats and Shelley [. . .] (*Town Talk*)[13]

> [Smith's] verse has more than a faint echo of that somewhat laboriously titanic poet, George Sterling. He has drunk too deeply of the "Wine of Wizardry" for one of his tender years. (Shaemas O'Sheel)[14]

- *His cosmic themes were a reflection of his youth and would soon be outgrown:*

> This Californian has extreme youth in his favor, so it would be idle to complain that his subjects are chiefly astronomic. Life will bring him down to earth, no doubt, in her usual brusque manner, and will teach him something more intimate to write about than winds and stars and forsaken gods. (Harriet Monroe)[15]

> To become serious, this youth has become superserious. He is overtrained [. . .] Hardly a note breathes of personal love or any such vivid adventurous life of the body and the blood as youth should have. [. . .] There are moments of youthful hysteria in the presence of great themes [. . .] (O'Sheel)[16]

- *His vocabulary presented a barrier to the average reader*

> [. . .] in a single stanza we find the words "vestitures," "emperies," and "susurrous," and the combined effect is almost cruel. The word "screed" would be fatal to any verse, and we shiver a little at the word "untremulous." The poet

---

13. "The Spectator," *Town Talk* (16 November 1912): 12.

14. Shaemas O'Sheel, "A Young Poet. He Has Quality, But Also the Faults of Youth," *New York Times Book Review* (26 January 1913); *FFT* 38.

15. [Harriet Monroe], "Recent Poetry," *Poetry* 2, No. 2 (April 1913); *FFT* 52.

16. O'Sheel, *FFT* 51.

would do well to view with extreme suspicion any word that is unusual, while anything that suggests a preference for unusual words or a search for them is apt to create a positive hostility in the mind of the reader. (*Argonaut*)[17]

[The poems] show his youth, his as yet unrealized value of simple words and phrases. . . . We are constantly confronted with such phrases as "intervital sleep," "systems triplicate," "anterior ones," "shuttles intricate of earth," "rapt in aural splendors ultimate" and "candent ores." (William Stanley Braithwaite)[18]

The first criticism of Smith's work, that it was overly influenced by Sterling, Keats, and others, and thus by implication or statement inferior to its precursors, reflects what Harold Bloom has termed "the anxiety of influence": all literary texts are strong misreadings of those that precede them, and it is the "strong poets, major figures [who] wrestle with their strong precursors, even to the death."[19] Even George Sterling later felt that this was a valid point, writing to a friend in 1925 that Smith was "hopelessly imitative, and at thirty has developed no style of his own [. . .] but can give you a replica of Baudelaire that is startling."[20] Sterling would go so far as to write a review of *Ebony and Crystal* (a collection to which he himself had written the preface), which he published in under the name of critic George Douglas, wherein he wrote that "Smith is a literary chameleon with a distressing facility for taking on the color of his poetic surroundings. At present these surroundings are Poe and Baudelaire with a little of George Sterling in the middle distance."[21] Yet it is apparent even at this stage of Smith's career that significant differences exist be-

---

17. "The Latest Books," *Argonaut* (30 November 1912): 365.

18. William Stanley Braithwaite, "Our Modern Poets," *Boston Evening Transcript* (2 April 1913); *FFT* 52. Poems cited: "Ode on Imagination," "Atlantis," and "The Unrevealed."

19. Harold Bloom, *The Anxiety of Influence*, 2nd ed. (New York: Oxford University Press, 1997), 5. Poems cited: "The Star-Treader," "Ode to Music," and "Ode on Imagination."

20. Henry Dumont, *Faun on Olympus* (unpublished manuscript, Library of Congress), 135.

21. George Sterling (as by "George Douglas"), "Recent Books of Fact and Fiction," [San Francisco] *Bulletin* (19 December 1922): 8.

Dead Reckonings

tween Smith and Sterling, Poe, and even Baudelaire. For instance, in *The Testimony of the Suns* Sterling presents personifications of the stars recounting their endless cycles of creation and destruction, whereas in "The Star-Treader," its counterpart or equivalent in Smith's collection, we see the unleashing of the *human* intelligence upon a cosmic stage. Not every reviewer felt that Smith's work was overly derivative. The unnamed reviewer for the *Wasp* wrote that "The remarkable feature of the verse of Clark Ashton Smith is that while it recalls the mannerisms of various poets, it has yet a native daring and distinctiveness marking an original outlook on the problems of man and the mysteries of nature," which reminds us of what Bloom wrote above.[22]

Early comparisons of Smith's work to that of Keats and Shelley were predicated upon the maturity of his work compared to that of those poets *at the same age*. As Sterling stated in various newspaper articles quoted above:

> Bryant wrote good poetry young, but it lacks the fire and splendor of Smith's; Keats and Shelley created poems at early ages, but they were of inferior workmanship; Rossetti wrote 'The Blessed Damozel' in his boyhood, but revised it later. I can find no poet who *at the age of 17* turned out such a poem as Smith's 'Saturn,' which, in my judgment, is in no way inferior to Keats' 'Hyperion.' And his 'Nero' is altogether astounding for a boy of 18."[23] (Emphasis added.)

Within these stated limitations, comparisons of the best of the early Smith with the early work of the great Romantic poets are not unreasonable.

However, Smith was particularly sensitive to criticism related to his age. He felt, perhaps correctly, that much of the attention focused upon him was of a kind with Doctor Johnson's observation about a woman preaching, namely that the wonder is not that it is done well but that it is done at all. He complained to Sterling that much that was written about him made him feel like

---

22. "Clark Ashton Smith, California Boy-Poet, Whose Muse Gives Promise of Masterpieces of Melody," *Wasp* (23 November 1912); *FFT* 39.

23. "Genius Flashes from the Sierras," 5.

"the human equivalent of a five-legged kangaroo."[24] It was probably for this reason that he rejected an otherwise positive review by the British poet Stephen Phillips and probably ignored a fine review by Arthur Machen.[25] And when *Town Talk* prefaced its review of *The Star-Treader* by describing Smith as "the Auburn boy for whom puberty and poetry were simultaneous phenomenon," who could blame him?[26]

There was, however, a glimmer of understanding here and there. Much had been made of Smith's isolated upbringing and limited education. Even Hopkins, a friend, pointed out that Smith preferred his own company to that of others; Ella J. Hamilton, wife of the Placer County District Attorney, wrote in a profile of Smith: "I wish I could picture to your mind the loneliness of this boy's life."[27] *The Star-Treader* abounds in images of the socially isolated individual: secluded forests, isolated mountaintops, the depths of interstellar space, etc. But the implication that his interest in cosmic subjects would fade as he attained maturity proved false. Porter Garnett, from whom we shall hear further, correctly classified Smith's work as following into two major categories: "In one his imagination transcends the limits of life and matter; in the other he clothes the things of earth in lyric beauty. There is, however, a third category, in which fall such poems as 'The Butterfly.' In this he applies the method of the first category to the material of the second. The poem is as aloof as 'The Star-Treader'."[28] Smith's cosmicism, his sense of the relative unimportance of mankind in the universal scheme of things, would only grow stronger as he grew older, but paradoxically his work would become more human as he began to treat his characters in a manner not entirely devoid of empathy or compassion. As E. Hoffmann Price observed in his memoir of Smith, the latter

---

24. Clark Ashton Smith, letter to George Sterling, September 7, 1912 (*SU* 60).

25. Stephen Phillips, "Voices from Overseas," *Poetry Review* 2 (1913): 141; Arthur Machen, "Books of Today," [London] *Evening News* (12 February 1916): 4.

26. "The Spectator," *Town Talk* (16 November 1912): 12.

27. Ella J. Hamilton (as "Mrs. G. K. Hamilton"), "A Poet and His Poetry. Clark Ashton Smith: Auburn's Gifted Youth," *Auburn Daily Journal* (27 March 1915): 1.

28. Porter Garnett, "A Young Poet and True," *San Francisco Call* (1 December 1912); *FFT* 37.

"portrayed human beings, not two dimensional and unconvincing simulacra which all too often rode unsteadily on a 'mood'."[29]

Treadwell's implication that Smith made up many of his words is not supported by an examination of the 1909 edition of *Webster's New International Dictionary* or the *Oxford English Dictionary*, both of which were available to Smith. Between them we may find not only even the most obscure word used in his early work, but also etymological discussions of the shades of meaning between words that would otherwise be synonyms. A careful reading of the poems shows that the objections of William Stanley Braithwaite are especially vulnerable to refutation, as witness his objection to the phrase "candent ore." As a brief phrase meant to summon up images of molten lava glowing in the depths of the earth, we can find no flaw with the term; one wonders if Mr. Braithwaite also objected to the term *incandescent lighting*? In reading these comments objecting to Smith's use of a wider vocabulary than the reviewer was wont to encounter, we are reminded of an observation made by Bierce in response to a similar criticism made of Sterling's "A Wine of Wizardry": "there are not a half-dozen words in the poem that are not in common use by good authors, and none that any man should not blush to say that he does not understand."[30] Bierce further opined: "Now, whose fault was it that this distinguished journalist had never heard of a gyre? Certainly not the poet's." For the *coup de grâce*, Bierce observed rather caustically that "A peasant is not to be censured for his ignorance, but when he glories in it and draws its limit as a deadline for his betters he is the least pleasing of all the beasts of the field."[31] If a person with aspirations toward culture cannot decipher words other than those of Anglo-Saxon derivation, the culprit most probably is to be found in a looking glass.

Let us examine more closely a few of the examples of which Sophie Treadwell made such sport. The phrase *frory beamlessness*

29. E. Hoffmann Price, *Book of the Dead: Friends of Yesteryear: Fictioneers and Others*, ed. Peter Ruber (Sauk City, WI: Arkham House, 2001), 125.

30. Ambrose Bierce, "An Insurrection of the Peasantry," in George Sterling, *Collected Poetry*, ed. S. T. Joshi and David E. Schultz (New York: Hippocampus Press, 2013), 2.700.

31. Ibid., 2.701.

may be found in Smith's poem "Lament of the Stars," which was included in *The Star-Treader*. While this is not a phrase found in everyday usage, its meaning is not difficult to understand. *Frory* means hoary or frost-covered, and *beamlessness* refers to the state of being without a beam or ray, i.e., of light. Here is the stanza in which this phrase appears:

> Beyond restrainless boundary-nights surpassing
> All luminous horizons limited,
> The substance and the light of her have fed
> Ruin and silence of the night's amassing:
> Abandoned worlds forever morningless;
> Suns without worlds, in frory beamlessness
> Girt for the longer gyre funereal;
> Inviolate silence, earless, unawaking
> That once was found, and level calm unbreaking
> Where motion's many ways in oneness fall
> Of sleep beyond forsaking.[32]

In context, a phrase that so succinctly suggests the frozen light-lessness of interstellar space, a realm completely devoid of any life or light, might be thought worthy of some little praise, but such was not the case.

Miss Treadwell's objection to the term *mystic immanence,* which Smith used in his "Ode to Music," is both perplexing and understandable, as "immanence" is a word commonly used in both philosophy and theology, albeit one that refers to a very difficult concept. (The phrase "mystic immanence" may be found in Taoist literature, which is possibly where Smith encountered it.) *Immanence* refers to that which dwells or remains inside something, although this is a gross simplification of a very complex idea. It is often used to refer to the idea of the Divine existing as part of creation as opposed to being outside of it. "Immanence" is an antonym of *transcendence*. In the context of Smith's poem, the term would then mean, very loosely, one's consciousness merging with the universe itself—an early instance of an idea to which Smith would return many times, most notably in *The*

---

32. Smith, "Lament of the Stars," *The Complete Poetry and Translations*, ed. S. T. Joshi and David E. Schultz (New York: Hippocampus Press, 2012), 1.101.

Hashish-Eater; or, The Apocalypse of Evil.

As for Treadwell's dismissal of Smith's style as "near Latin," she would not be the last writer to take him to task for this, but all who did so failed to recognize that this was, in contemporary parlance, more of a feature than a bug. Many years later Smith would explain his choices in some detail in a letter to a friend:

> As to my own employment of an ornate style, using many words of classic origin and exotic color, I can only say that [it] is designed to produce effects of language and rhythm which could not possibly be achieved by a vocabulary restricted to what is known as "basic English." As Strachey points out, a style composed largely of words of Anglo-Saxon origin tends to a spondaic rhythm, "which by some mysterious law, reproduces the atmosphere of ordinary life." An atmosphere of remoteness, vastness, mystery and exoticism is more naturally evoked by a style with an admixture of Latinity, lending itself to more varied and sonorous rhythms, as well as to subtler shades, tints and nuances of meaning—all of which, of course, are wasted or worse on the average reader, even if presumably literate.[33]

It is not surprising that Smith's vocabulary would not meet with a friendly reception at the dawn of literary Modernism.

Smith also found himself being criticized for the "morbidity" of his work, which not surprising when we remember that Poe's own position in the literary canon was by no means secure in 1912 and unpleasant or "ugly" subject matter was shunned by genteel people. "G. R. Y." wrote in a review that "Smith has a terrific imagination, and not unfrequently he allows it to lead him off into the horrible."[34] John Jury, the book reviewer for the *San Jose Mercury,* did not care for Smith's attitude: "In respect to the view of life and nature taken by the author of 'The Star Treader,' I must confess to a feeling of great disappointment. The thought is constantly borne in upon me in reading the lines that an undue and sinister emphasis is placed upon the thoughts of chaos, of in-

---

33. Smith, letter to Samuel J. Sackett, 11 July 1950; in *Selected Letters of Clark Ashton Smith,* ed. David E. Schultz and Scott Connors (Sauk City, WI: Arkham House, 2003), 365 (hereafter *SL*).

34. G. R. Y., "Clark Ashton Smith and His Book of Verse," uncredited newspaper clipping, A. M. Robertson Papers, Bancroft Library (*FFT* 42).

direction, of death. Adjectives depicting the hideous, the ghoulish, the destructive, and the seemingly brutal in nature are overworked."[35] He was particularly offended by Smith's sonnet "Retrospect and Forecast," which he called a "libel upon the nature of life which is given the character of a vampire."[36] Despite these reservations about Smith's collection, Jury was nonetheless "impressed with its maturity of thought and its opulence in language."[37]

This is not to say that Smith did not receive his share of accolades or favorable reviews. The Irish-American poet Shaemas O'Sheel, writing in the *New York Times Book Review,* expressed the reservations quoted above, but he also expressed the opinion that "what makes us say that there is at last to be a poet by the name of Smith is, that the best poems in the book are astonishingly splendid and majestic treatments of cosmic themes, in a style of high and radiant rhetoric."[38] Porter Garnett, a librarian at the University of California at Berkeley, recalled the furor of the past summer in the first lines of his review for the *San Francisco Call:* "The emergence of a true poet usually excites an interest which is more general than genuine. Clark Ashton Smith [. . .] is a true poet. He is a truer poet than we had any right to infer from the examples of his which have appeared in the news columns of the daily press in advance of their publication." Garnett exhibited considerable understanding of Smith's work: in his work the young poet "takes an external view of the material universe, looking in from space like a 'curious god.'"[39] Similar observations have been made by many commentators, but Porter Garnett has the distinction of being the first.

Even reviewers who were generally unfavorable toward Smith's themes or treatments had good things to say about his overall work. William Stanley Braithwaite thought that "the substance of a very fine poet is in Mr. Smith. He has displayed in

---

35. John Jury, "The Star-Treader, A Book of Verse by Clark Ashton Smith," *San Jose Mercury and Herald* (8 December 1912); *FFT* 47.

36. *FFT* 48.

37. *FFT* 46.

38. O'Sheel, *FFT* 51.

39. Garnett, *FFT* 37. The phrase "curious god" occurs in "The Star-Treader."

this book imagination enough to stock a good many poets."[40] The reviewer for *Poetry* praised his "unusual imaginative power of visualizing these remote splendors until they have the concrete definiteness of a personal experience"—high praise indeed for the flagship of the literary movement that called itself "Imagism."[41]

One surprisingly favorable review appeared in the San Francisco *Bulletin*. Herbert Bashford (an old literary foe of Bierce and Sterling) praised Smith's poems highly, calling his review "Wonderful Lyrics Deserve Recognition with World's Best." After praising "Nero" as "tremendously powerful and imaginative," Bashford predicted that "he will one day be numbered among the greatest of the world's geniuses, despite the fact that he was born a poet in an intensely materialistic age. Such poetry as his cannot fail to arouse the admiration of mankind sometime."[42]

Alas, Clark Ashton Smith made his debut when the "Genteel Tradition" was still staggering along, and the literary revolutionaries led by Ezra Pound were first making themselves felt. Years later Smith would write that he felt more like an outsider than his late friend H. P. Lovecraft, because "his 'outsideness' was principally in regard to time-period; mine is one of space, too."[43] Smith found himself caught between Scylla and Charybdis: too unconventional for the status quo, but too traditional for the avant garde. But as Smith wrote in a letter thanking Bashford for his review, "Poetry, particularly work like mine, which is so far removed from the everyday interest of the immense bulk of mankind, stands in little danger of being overestimated in these days. Therefore I am so much the more grateful for your appreciation, and desirous of thanking you for it."[44]

---

40. Braithwaite, *FFT* 52.

41. [Monroe], *FFT* 52.

42. Herbert Bashford, "The Latest in Literature," [San Francisco] *Bulletin* (30 November 1912): 14.

43. Smith, letter to R. H. Barlow, 16 May 1937 (*SL* 302).

44. Smith, letter to Herbert Bashford, 15 January 1913 (*SL* 18).

Who Is Dr. Prozess?

S. T. Joshi

MARK SAMUELS. *The Prozess Manifestations*. Düsseldorf: Zagava, 2017. 135 pp. €49 (numbered edition), €268 (lettered edition).

One of my keenest regrets as a critic of weird fiction is that I have not kept up with the work of the British writer Mark Samuels. I read and greatly enjoyed one of his early story collections, *The White Hands and Other Weird Tales* (2003), but have failed to read the half-dozen volumes he has published in the interim, among them *Glyphotech* (2008; published in an expanded edition in 2016), *The Man Who Collected Machen* (2010), and *Written in Darkness* (2014). Thankfully, several of these volumes—initially published in expensive and limited hardcover editions—are becoming available in more affordable reprints. And the timely appearance of the volume under review provides an appropriate occasion for an overview of Samuels's work.

No less an authority than Ramsey Campbell, in his introduction to the original edition of *Glyphotech,* deemed Samuels one of the two "modern masters" of "urban weirdness"—the other being Thomas Ligotti. High praise, indeed! (But it is difficult to imagine Campbell himself, author of *The Face That Must Die,* "Mackintosh Willy," and so many other great tales of urban horror, not being cited in this context.) Campbell also points out the ways in which Samuels draws upon the work of Lovecraft, Hodgson, and other classic writers without in any way descending into mechanical pastiche. The present volume, for all its slenderness—it only contains six stories—highlights a number of the same points.

For a writer who seems devoted to "classic" weird fiction, the opening story in the book ("Decay") is not at all what one would expect. Here we see Samuels finding the source of weirdness in the most cutting-edge products of our overly technological age. A man named Riaz is tasked by a company named Hermes X with conducting surveillance on one Cornelius Parry, who seems to have valuable information on computers or AI or some such thing. When Riaz finally contrives to enter Parry's apartment in Brooklyn, he finds that "It was like stepping into a vast mechanical brain." The course of the narrative makes ominously clear what Parry has done with his knowledge of AI—knowledge that may be draining human beings of their own grasp on knowledge and reality.

Not quite as successful is "Moon Blood-Red, Tide Turning," in which an unnamed narrator recalls working for a play publisher when he was a young man, and there encountering a young actress named Celia Waters. She leaves the company to act in a play called *New Quests for Nothing,* by "Doctor Prozess," to be performed in a theatre in Cornwall. The various bizarre manifestations that occur during and after the play's performance create an interesting atmosphere of bizarrerie, but do not quite cohere into a comprehensible unity.

"An End to Perpetual Motion" is set on a transatlantic liner in the late 1920s, where the playwright Ambrose Hamilton encounters a mysterious figure named Ignatius Zeno. Zeno seems to be constantly circling the globe, as if he were determined never to remain still. When the ship unexpectedly comes to a stop in the course of its voyage, we learn to our terror why Zeno was inclined toward perpetual motion.

Two vaguely related stories at the end of the book are extraordinary ventures into hallucinatory prose and imagery. "Court of Midnight" tells of a poet named Melchior who seeks out the court in question because he is hoping to consult Dr. Prozess for a cure of his "lunar fever." Along the way he meets a fellow poet, Santon, who is hideously mutilated:

> His face was a travesty of the human. Fully half was corroded away by craters, revealing the skull beneath. Never before have I seen such white, leprous skin, colourless like alabaster. How terrible were the depths of his wholly black eyes! They stared, devoid of all intelligence, like holes pressed into putty.

It is to be questioned whether even Dr. Prozess can cure such ills.

The next tale, "In the Complex," creates an even more effective atmosphere of the strange, set in a hospital where the narrator is being treated (apparently by Dr. Prozess) for an unspecified ailment. As the narrator is systematically degraded, both physically and psychologically, by those who are ostensibly treating him, we seem to have descended into an inescapable and Kafkaesque *conte cruel*.

The fleeting mentions of Dr. Prozess in all but one of the stories is an interesting effect (rather similar to the citations of the elusive James Harris in many tales in Shirley Jackson's *The Lottery* [1949]), but I am not sure they fully cohere. Perhaps they are not meant to; and the author makes clear his desire to keep the baleful doctor in the background as a sinister figure—or, perhaps, a symbol of all the incomprehensible horror that lies behind the surface of life.

The one story that does not mention Prozess—and the longest in the book—is "The Crimson Fog," and it would justify purchase of this volume all on its own. This superb excursion into Lovecraftian cosmic horror tells of an expedition to the disputed province of Chang-Yi, evidently lying on the border between Russia and China. Other expeditions have disappeared there, especially in the wake of a crimson fog that has engulfed the area and (like the gray dust of "The Colour out of Space") is spreading little by little. Moreover, there are unknown entities in the fog-ridden region that exhibit an unnerving taste for human flesh. When the narrator, Sloan, goes into the area with several other individuals, including the translator Yian-Ho, to find a Lieutenant Qersh, who had gone there earlier but from whom nothing had been heard since, the adventure begins. It would be criminal to reveal the details of the meticulously worked-out plot, where one by one the members of the expedition suffer horrible deaths (one is left as a "sickening trail of human jam"). Suffice it to say that the narrator's realization of the true state of affairs elicits cosmic reflections on his part:

And thoughts I had thought before, not long ago, came back to me. Reality tearing itself apart at the seams as the cosmos expands. What lies beyond the edge of the visible universe cannot be known. The distance is greater than what light itself, or any other form of radiation, can reveal. The crimson fog—existence itself is bleeding to death.

This story contains a number of sly references to Lovecraftian elements, not least of which is the figure of Yian-Ho (although in Lovecraft's tales this is a place, not a person). Other tales carry on the practice: Parry, in "Decay," lives at 169 Clinton Street in Brooklyn Heights, where Lovecraft himself spent a miserable year and a quarter in 1925–26; and Dr. Prozess concludes "Court of Midnight" with a laconic telegram that ends: "EXPECT GREAT REVELATIONS." It would take an experienced Lovecraftian to recall that this is exactly what the alien entity disguising itself as Henry Wentworth Akeley, in a telegram of its own, tells Albert N. Wilmarth (in "The Whisperer in Darkness") as a way of luring Wilmarth up to Akeley's isolated cabin in Vermont.

But in-jokes of this sort are not what make Mark Samuels's stories so powerful. He has a sure grasp of the psychology of terror, knowing exactly what hints and details are likely to trigger in the reader the sense of unease and "wrongness" that is the essence of the weird. His prose is fluid, richly textured, and at times hypnotic, whether he is dealing with contemporary phenomena or those of the historical past. A number of the stories in this book have a kind of European ambiance, recalling the themes and atmosphere of such writers as Jean Ray and Stefan Grabinski. But they nonetheless remain highly original, reflecting Samuels's own concerns about our hapless position in a universe we cannot hope to understand and enmeshed in societal norms that are just as incomprehensible.

This superbly produced book, containing "visual interpretations" of Samuels's writing by the artist Ibrahim R. Ineke, is a pleasure in itself. Even if the copy editing is not quite what it could be, it is an exquisite example of bookmaking. The print run is highly limited (170 numbered and 26 lettered copies), so let us hope that the publisher decides to issue the book in a more accessible edition. It, and Samuels's work in general, deserve the widest possible readership.

Dreams of a Particular Place

Géza A. G. Reilly

KARIN TIDBECK. *Jagannath*. New York: Vintage Books, 2018. 176 pp. $16.00 tpb. ISBN: 978-1-101-97397-4.

There is a specific charm, I think, in being able to read stories whose genesis depends upon a culture alien to one's own. *Jagannath,* Karin Tidbeck's collection of short stories, could not have been written (or, at least, could not have been written as it has been) if Tidbeck had been born in North America or the United Kingdom rather than in her native Sweden. Reading her stories is, for me, akin to eagerly peeking through a previously locked doorway leading into a secret room. What one sees therein is not always pretty, but it is always fascinating.

This quality of peeking in on the hidden and the secret is doubled in Tidbeck's work, since her stories often hinge upon events in a world that cannot be anticipated or easily defined. Her stories are perhaps the worthiest of the generic label of "fantastic" that I have encountered in some time; trying to pigeonhole them into more specific genres (such as magical realism, horror, or fantasy) would be doing them a disservice. Whether we are discussing "Beatrice," where a doctor falls in love with an airship and a young woman falls in love with a steam engine, or "Reindeer Mountain," where a family's history of mental illness might hint at a darker element in their makeup, or the eponymous "Jagannath," where stunted humans pilot a giant creature that may be the world itself, Tidbeck's fiction consistently investigates the liminal space between the impossible and the real in a way that never grows tiresome.

That Tidbeck does so by utilizing the mythological culture of her homeland only adds to the quality of her tales, allowing her to draw upon her own soil to the betterment of her aesthetic craft. Regionalist critic Michael Kowalewski, following after Pierre Sansot, notes that rather than asking after the "essence of a place" we should be concerned with "what can one dream about it" (*Reading the West,* 1996), and that is precisely what Tidbeck has asked of her homeland in the process of writing these stories: not what life in Sweden is like in a prosaic sense, but what dreams about Sweden the author can discover. These dreams sometimes involve versions of the *vittra,* what we in North America might term elves or fairies or trolls, or they might involve more outré beings that are nevertheless steeped in Swedish life and culture. Stories like "Brita's Holiday Village" and "Some Letters for Ove Lindström" are especially indebted to Tidbeck's dreams of Nordic mythology and Swedish life, and it is these stories (among others) that make this collection truly shine.

And yet, not everything in *Jagannath* revolves around simple themes of re-envisioning mythology or the "liminal sense of transcending borders" (as Elizabeth Hand phrases it in her foreword to the collection). I was surprised, for example, by how many stories involved themes of family and parenthood or childhood, such as "Beatrice," "Cloudberry Jam," "Miss Nyberg and I," and even the excellent "Pyret." As with her more regional stories, Tidbeck constructs these works with deftness, nuance, and care that removes any of the potential sting caused by an inability to suspend our disbelief. I would not be so crass as to suggest that there is an overall ur-meaning to Tidbeck's stories about or involving family, but I will say that she seems to be hinting that family and child/parent relationships are more complicated—and often more monstrous—than we might normally imagine.

What is truly shocking, however, is that so many of Tidbeck's stories are pulled off without a hitch. Even "Rebecka," a seemingly easy story of survival and dismay, carries with it haunting overtones bound to stay with readers of a certain type long after the story has ended. Indeed, out of the thirteen stories in *Jagannath,* only a few are disappointing. "Who Is Arvid Pekon?" (also the title of the Swedish version of *Jagannath: Vem är Arvid Pekon?*), for example, simply falls down in execution—though I fully admit that there might be a cultural difference causing the story to come off as a clunker in my reading. Equally, "Herr Cederberg" is an inoffensive enough tale, but too (perhaps ironically) light and breezy for my liking. And the grotesque "Aunts" strikes me as thoroughly unnecessary despite having some of the most striking—and most visceral—imagery among the stories.

But these are minor flaws from what is otherwise an outstanding collection, and I would not dream of suggesting that readers skip over these few missteps in the path laid out for us.

Especially since Tidbeck's prose is clean, sharp, and entirely engaging throughout. Though not without nuance, her prose is totally lacking in muddy or fuzzy stylistics, making each story a straightforward read without sacrificing subtlety or aesthetic beauty. The prose in *Jagannath* is all the more noteworthy because Tidbeck chose to translate her stories into English herself (a difficult process that she discusses in her afterword to the collection). Translation, as anyone who has read Umberto Eco's novels post–William Weaver can attest to, is a finicky thing. Had anyone other than Tidbeck translated her stories, I am not certain that they would carry the same weight or move with the same energy that they do. I am certain, however, that they would not have shied away from attempting to translate the *concept* of "dansband" into English, as Tidbeck wisely refuses to do, and perhaps would have mangled the oft-repeated delightful translation of so-and-so "smiled with both rows of teeth."

Overall, *Jagannath* is not a collection that is going to set the world on fire. But that is all right, because I do not think that it wishes to do so. What it does do is provide a peek into a world kept secret from many of us in North America, and to present, without pretension, an author's unique perspective on that world. In our current state of theme anthologies and collections without poise or originality, Karin Tidbeck's *Jagannath* is a breath of fresh air. Hers is a voice that I am glad exists, and it is one that I hope to hear whispering to me again as the sun sets slowly over the mountains. *Jagannath* is available as of this writing from Vintage Books in physical format and on the US Amazon and Barnes & Noble sites in ebook format. We should all read it and stay awhile, wandering on Tidbeck's imaginative soil.

Dreams of the House of the Worm: Gary Myers's Debut Dreamlands Story

Nicholas Diak

H. P. Lovecraft's Cthulhu Mythos has been a fertile playground for aspiring writers to pen their own Lovecraftian stories, pastiches, and continuations for numerous decades. While stories, both short and novel-length, featuring elements from this mythos are plentiful, one is hard pressed to see such adaptation from his Dunsanian Dreamlands body of work. There are a handful of authors who write within Lovecraft's Dreamlands: Brian Lumley is perhaps the best-known, having written many books in that setting during the '80s starting with *Hero of Dreams,* while Kij Johnson is the most recent, having re-imagined much of the Dreamlands in her novella *The Dream-Quest of Vellitt Boe.*

Singularly, however, perhaps the most important author who pioneered the Dreamlands canon is Gary Myers. Myers's short story collection *The House of the Worm* (originally published in 1975) is the first foundational Dreamlands text post-Lovecraft upon which successor writers have since built. Myers's contributions to the Dreamlands, such as new cities, deities, geographies, and so on, have been absorbed into Chaosium's *Dreamlands* supplement for the *Call of Cthulhu* role-playing game, which not only further canonized Myers's work but helped proliferate his addenda to a wider audience. Comic book writer and artist Jason Bradley Thompson has even incorporated Myers's work into the various extravagant maps that adorn his graphic novels and posters.

Despite his contributions to the Dreamlands, Myers remains more of a cult figure when compared to other authors who write in the Lovecraftian vein; he is important, but not as well known or revered. The purpose of this essay is to provide a better appreciation and understanding of Myers by examining his first short story, "The House of the Worm," and its various incarnations and changes over the years. Three distinct versions of "The House of the Worm" have been published during Myers's career, and a closer look at these versions will provide not only insight into Myers's creative process but also illumination into outside factors that have shaped these texts. This essay will compare and contrast the three versions of "The House of the Worm." Contextualization for "The House of the Worm" is provided by quotations from Myers himself.

Versioning History and Synopsis of "The House of the Worm"

Written at the age of sixteen, "The House of the Worm" was Myers's first published story. It caught the attention of August Derleth when Myers included a draft of the story with a book order to Arkham House (Thompson) and was subsequently published in the *Arkham Collector* No. 7 (Summer 1970) and reprinted in the *Arkham Collector, Volume 1* the next year (Joshi 108–9, 128). The story also appeared in Lin Carter's anthology *New Worlds for Old* in 1971. The second version of "The House of the Worm" appears as the lead-off story in Myers's collection *The House of the Worm*, published by Arkham House in 1975, while the final, canonical version appears in Myers's collection *The Country of the Worm: Excursions Beyond the Wall of Sleep* in 2013. While the text of "The House of the Worm" is finalized in *The Country of the Worm*, the collection itself has seen additional stories continuously added to it.

The titular House of the Worm stands at the center of five stone pillars atop a hill outside the town of Vornai on the Plains of Kaar.[1] One hundred years ago, the Old Man of Whom No One Likes to Speak constructed the House overnight, causing much fearful speculation from the Vornai townsfolk. On his hundredth year of residency, he sends out invitations to the citizens of Vornai to join him in a series of nightly banquets. A group of young men accept this offer, and each night they dine in a pentagon-shaped room, drinking wine as the Old Man of Whom No One Likes to Speak regales them with dark secrets. Each night, fewer men return to the banquets, until at last only three guests remain. On this final night, the Old Man confesses that he is a custodian of a Seal of the Elder Gods—the five stone pillars that the House sits between. He leads his guests into the

---

1. The *Dreamlands* supplement for the *Call of Cthulhu* RPG places Vornai far north near Inganok, the city made of onyx through which Randolph Carter passes in *The Dream-Quest of Unknown Kadath*.

tunnels that run deep and dark under the House to a mammoth pit containing a monstrous evil that the Old Man is always on guard for or against. As the pipes and flutes that keep Azathoth asleep fill the chamber, an entity reaches up from the pit and pulls the Old Man inside.

Textual Alterations and Edits

Between the three versions of "The House of the Worm," numerous edits, corrections, and omissions can be found. The first notable difference is the presence of introductory and concluding paragraphs in the original version in *New Worlds for Old* but omitted from *The House of the Worm* and *The Country of the Worm*. The introductory paragraph overtly establishes that the story takes place in the Dreamlands, as the narrator, a dreamer, mentions traversing the seventy steps and the caverns of flame while making callbacks to prior adventures in Ulthar, Celephaïs, and Kadath in the Cold Waste. While the *House/Country of the Worm* editions end with the Old Man of Whom No One Likes to Speak being pulled into the pit, the original version continues with several more paragraphs. In these additional paragraphs, Betelgeuse winks out of existence and the pillars that make up the Seal of the Elder Gods surrounding the house topple. The dreamer, much like Randolph Carter in "The Silver Key," appears to have lost the ability to enter the Dreamlands, which are now under the rule of the Great Old Ones.

The original rationale for the introductory and concluding paragraphs was that Myers had written his story to be a standalone adventure:

> . . . all the choices I made in it were based on that assumption. Since I was setting it in Lovecraft's Dreamworld, I thought I had better say so up front. Since I had no intention of revisiting that world, I thought it might be fun to destroy it at the end. But I had to rethink both these choices after I sold the story to August Derleth's Arkham House and a series became a real possibility. If I was not going to begin every story by trumpeting its locality, then why begin even one that way? And if I destroyed the world in the first story, wouldn't that hamper me in writing a second?

So out they both went.[2]

Another source of difference between "The House of the Worm" incarnations is Myers's renaming or recasting of both his own elements and those of Lovecraft. For example, the original version in *New Worlds for Old* contains a handful of references to Lovecraft's Pnakotic Manuscripts, but *The Country of the Worm* contains only one. The mention of Nyarlathotep from the original version is omitted from *The House/Country of the Worm* versions. The deities that Myers introduces also go through different name changes. For example, the god Nsekmbl, introduced in the original version, is changed to N'tse-Kaambl in *The House of the Worm* and changed once more to Djin-Mah-Kwee in *The Country of the Worm.*

Myers's initial take on these alterations (from the story's original version to its second) can be found in the introduction to *The House of the Worm,* where Myers states that his creations are purposely both "very far from Derleth, but also from the Cthulhu Mythos proper" (*House of the Worm* viii). However, with additional changes between the second version and the final, canonical version of the story, Myers revises his rationale:

> In those days the Derlethian model of the Cthulhu Mythos (a name Derleth coined) was still dominant. This has been characterized as a quasi-Christian struggle of good against evil. That is probably an over-simplification, but the effect is still the same: If Cthulhu breaks free of his watery tomb, some greater entity appears and seals him back up again. Either way, it has little to do with the Lovecraftian model, which is a bleaker, more hopeless affair. I think I must always have sensed this difference, and when the Lovecraftian writer Richard L. Tierney published an article laying it out in black and white, I was bowled over by its obvious truth. In a direct response to Tierney's article I recast the mythological background of my story to reflect my new understanding, wrote an introduction to justify what I had done, and included them both in my 1975 collection. So far, so good. But when, some twenty years later, I had occasion to revisit that book, two things struck me. One was, that the Derleth controversy was over

2. Gary Myers, email message to author, 7 October 2015. Sincere appreciation and gratitude to Myers for participating in the interview that would become this essay.

Dead Reckonings

and done. And the other was, that the rewriting I had done in the service of that controversy did not really fit my story. So I restored it, as I said before, to something closer to its original Derlethian form. My vast reading public did not lose much by this. My mythological innovations can still be read to better effect in a story called "The Snout in the Alcove." But I had learned a valuable lesson. You can change a story for artistic reasons and all will be well. But if you change it for didactic ones, you do so at your peril.[3]

A final, more practical change between the original version of "The House of the Worm" and later versions is the adjustment of the passage of time. In the original, the feasts unfold over many months while in *The House/Country of the Worm* versions they occur over several nights. Per Myers:

> Pacing is certainly part of it. I do think that brevity and simplicity are important auctorial virtues, though my writing may not always show it. But I also think the change improves the internal logic of the story. How long could the Old Man reasonably expect to keep the same guests coming back for the same old entertainment?[4]

While the vast majority of changes that have occurred in "The House of the Worm" through the different versions were implemented by Myers himself, there is one change that occurred without his consent, and that is the alteration of the title to "The Feast in the House of the Worm," made by Lin Carter for the anthology *New Worlds for Old*. According to Myers, the text of "The Feast in the House of the Worm" is identical to its counterparts in the two *Arkham Collector* editions save for the title.[5] Myers provided some insight in regard to his working relationship with Carter in an interview with Jason Thompson for the *Lovecraft eZine:* he held Carter in high regard for the second life he gave to obscure stories through reprints in the Ballantine Adult Fantasy Series and the esteem he himself received by appearing in that series, but Myers did not know when a story of his was going to be reprinted in the series until he happened upon it in published form, and many times he was not compensated unless he queried

---

3. Myers, email.

4. Ibid.

5. Ibid.

Carter for payment (Thompson). In regard to "The House of the Worm," the title change was executed without Myers's permission or prior knowledge by Carter. Though Myers is not privy to the reasons behind the change, he remains nonplussed by the alteration: "there are far worse things awaiting the aspiring fantasy writer than being picked up by the legendary editor of the Ballantine Adult Fantasy Series."[6] In the long run, the title change seems fairly innocuous, with little impact to the meaning of Myers's text proper, but it does provide insight into Carter and how he operated as an editor. Carter's enthusiasm and good intentions with his anthologies are certainly manifest, even if at times some of his actions were taken without consent from his writers.

Dark Motives

As illustrated above, the prior four decades have seen a variety of alterations to the text of "The House of the Worm," but the core of the story remains unchanged: an old man entertains guests in his house and meets his end by an unseen creature in the tunnels below. The passage of time, however, can bring new reflection and interpretation to the text, especially from the text's creator. The plot of "The House of the Worm" begs a fundamental question: why is the Old Man of Whom No One Likes to Speak hosting these banquets? Overtly, the text states that "whether because he desired company or for some darker reason, an invitation to dine that evening at the old man's sinister House was found one morning tacked to the front door of every house in the city" (*Country of the Worm* 6). This rationale has remained textually consistent in both the *New Worlds for Old* and *House of the Worm* iterations of the story as well. Off the page, however, Myers has noted that the Old Man's motives are somewhat more complex:

> If you had asked me it forty years ago, I probably would have answered that he wanted company. Nowadays, though, I would point to his motives as one of my darker Lovecraftian shadings. Put it this way. Suppose you knew, absolutely knew, that the world was ending tomorrow at noon and there was nothing, absolutely nothing, that you or anyone else could do to stop it. Would you keep the knowledge to yourself so that everyone else

---

6. Myers, email.

could go out in blissful ignorance? Or would you shout it from the housetops and throw everyone else into as big a panic as you? But never mind what you would do. What would the typical Lovecraftian first-person narrator/protagonist do? I submit that my Old Man is descended, however distantly, from these.[7]

There is, of course, some dark irony in Myers's example of the world ending, as he had excised the world-ending conclusion from the original version of "The House of the Worm." Yet the Old Man is still the keeper of a dark secret that can end the world (he is the jailer of something insidious), and his series of banquets, complete with much wine consumption, is his way of working up the courage to share his secret with the hardy men from Vornai. After all, would he not need a successor at some point? With the Old Man of Whom No One Likes to Speak pulled into the pit, the world may not have immediately ended, but the machinations to its end have certainly been jump-started. The jailed entities over which he was a custodian are now certainly on the loose, and their exploits can be witnessed in Myers's next story, "Yohk the Necromancer."

In a grander scheme of things, "The House of the Worm" has become the starting point of many trajectories. The narrative proper led to additional stories in Myers's body of work (as can be seen in his collections), which in turn became the backbone of successor stories written by other Dreamlands authors (no doubt due in part to its canonization through the *Dreamlands* RPG supplement). The comparison of the various versions of the story with Myers's contextualization provides not only insight into Myers's creative process, but also gives additional illumination into the environment in which Lovecraftian writers of the time operated. "The House of the Worm," through its different incarnations, has become a critical, important, and essential text within the greater Lovecraftian canon.

Bibliography

Joshi, S. T. *Sixty Years of Arkham House*. Sauk City, WI: Arkham House Publishers, 1999.

---

7. Ibid.

Lovecraft, H. P. (writer), and Jason Bradley Thompson (artist). *The Dream-Quest of Unknown Kadath & Other Stories*. Seattle, WA: Mock Man Press. 2011.

Myers, Gary. "The Feast in the House of the Worm." In *New Worlds for Old,* edited by Lin Carter. New York: Ballantine Books, 1971. 154–63.

———. "The House of the Worm." In *The Country of the Worm: Excursions Beyond the Wall of Sleep*. n.p.: CreateSpace, 2013.

———. *The House of the Worm*. Sauk City, WI: Arkham House, 1975.

Thompson, Jason. "Spawn of Dark Dreams: An Interview with Gary Myers." *Lovecraft eZine*. Last modified 25 September 2013. https://lovecraftzine.com/2013/09/25/spawn-of-dark-dreams-an-interview-with-gary-myers-by-jason-thompson/.

Ramsey's Rant: Honoured by Horror

Ramsey Campbell

It has been the best part of sixty years since I sent some imitation Lovecraft tales to August Derleth to find out if he thought they were any good. I never expected Arkham House to publish them, let alone what followed. August Derleth's encouragement and editorial advice helped inspire me to create cosmic creatures of my own. I was touched and honoured when one of those entities spawned an anthology in tribute, *The Children of Gla'aki*, and I wrote an afterword to the book, having elsewhere revived the spiny chap myself in a novella (*The Last Revelation of Gla'aki*) meant to improve on the treatment I'd dealt him when I was sixteen years old. As if this anthology weren't enough of an accolade, Scott David Aniolowski and Joseph S. Pulver Sr have compiled a book of tales based on the range of my career, *Darker Companions*. I didn't see that one until PS published it, and I hope folk won't find me too intolerably self-indulgent if I muse about it here.

The opening surprise comes in Scott's introduction, where he mentions that he and Joe originally thought of editing an anthology based on my first Lovecraftian book. Apparently, he and Joe were unaware that a compilation of the kind was already in the works. How would two such uncanny twins have looked? Even the Whateleys might have been proud, but I'm prouder to have influenced the tales I read.

Michael Wehunt takes first place with "Holoow" and swiftly seizes my imagination with images I wish I'd written: "the buildings held a rail of sky like a vise," "the low-bellied bed" . . . These days many of my characters have aged along with me, but I was writing oldsters more than half my life ago, and Wehunt enters at least as sympathetically into such a protagonist. It's an unsparingly honest portrait, but a compassionate one, and its growing paranoia is undoubtedly authentic. This merges with a sense of the urban uncanny until they grow indistinguishable from each other, and there are hints of their psychological basis. Long ago I concluded that an enigma can be more fruitful than any explanation, and such a tale confirms my conviction.

I still recall my delight in reading Steve Rasnic Tem's "City Fishing," which I bought for *New Terrors* many years ago. His story in the present book, "The Long Fade into Evening" might describe our elderly state, though Steve shows no sign of creative fading, and I hope I don't just yet. His ageing protagonist seems beset by a new world too strange to be entirely real, let alone re-assuring. Is that Mackintosh Willy's relative on the bus? The trav-eller has horrid characteristics all of its own. At times, I feel as if I'm imagining the present book—having one of my recurrent dreams in which I return to a bookshop remembered from a pre-vious dream and find strange volumes I leaf through but never buy before I wake. In Steve's tale, not just a house but an entire dis-trict feels uneasily haunted, not to say informed by its new ten-ant's history—indeed, alive in its own relentlessly unnerving way. Eventually it burgeons into a nightmare I might have had myself (an experience I first had in the eighties, reading Russell Flinn's fine "Subway Story," which read like a tale I'd forgotten I wrote).

In S. P. Miskowski's "Asking Price" a house summarises a family, and nostalgia is progressively corroded by glimpses of the truth. Like many of my characters, her protagonist is beset by in-troversion, but the narrative only very gradually reveals the dark-ness at its core. If this house is haunted spectrally as well as psychologically, it hardly needs to be. I'm struck by how the tale recalls a number of mine in a general way but remains very much its author's and itself.

Whenever we and our friends the Proberts get together much fun ensues, and there's plenty in John Llewellyn Probert's contri-bution "Author? Author!," starting with the allusive first line. In-deed, he read the story to us before publication to make sure I approved. I more than do. Look for some naughty knowing ref-erences as well as many to my stories, but is this only comedy? To what extent does a writer's fiction remake the world or at least some readers' view of it, not to mention his own? Or does he tell tales because of the world, to convey his view of it? On quite a few occasions I've felt I was inhabiting my own fiction—most re-cently, when on the last leg of my journey back from Seoul to Manchester, the airport security equipment refused to confirm I existed. Perhaps that's how the long fade into evening begins.

In Michael Griffin's "Meriwether" ominous British influences shape an American coastal village. To what extent are the elements mine? The man's obsession with a bookshop could be, and the engagement that won't last, and the increasing ambiguity and unreliability of language. At the same time Griffin reaches for weirdness and awe in a strikingly personal way, and his story has its own highly individual existence.

Alison Littlewood's "The Entertainment Arrives" homes in on a favourite setting of mine—the seaside resort out of season. I suspect it may have resonance for her as well, and it demonstrates her enviable talent for evoking Northern locations. Ambiguities abound: the way a car behaves, or a hotel sign, or the smell of rain, not to say the name and nature of the performer whose thoughts we share. If he's the source of terror, he's its victim too. While the title recalls one of mine, the story is a decidedly original variation on "The Entertainment," and conjures up its own dark myth.

Marc Laidlaw is another veteran of *New Terrors*, and the Daliesque horror that ends his tale of forty years ago haunts me still. "Premonition" is as succinct as I once was and wish I could be more often. Sunshine and crowds offer no reassurance in this story; they simply bring the terror into sharper focus. As elsewhere in this book, I have the unsettling sense that a contributor has reached deep into my mind and found one of my persistent fears. Whenever Jenny swims in the sea I can't relax until she returns to the beach, since I'm unable to swim. Once she and our son (then a youngster) swam in a fierce Turkish river, from which I'm sure swimmers would be banned by the authorities now. Yet the nightmare Marc has brought me here is more terrible still.

In "A Perfect Replica" Damien Angelica Walters unites two elements I've often depended upon: a child's viewpoint, modulating the prose to convey it, and the example of M. R. James—the artefact that becomes instinct with the spectral. Recall James's mezzotint and his haunted doll's house, but the contents of the item in Damien's tale aren't bounded by the item they inhabit. Terror can be poignant, indeed moving, and I submit her tale as powerful evidence.

Gary McMahon's "There, There" begins innocuously enough, which ought to be fair warning that we're bound for darker things, especially in Gary's case. The protagonist swiftly grows as isolated as any of my loners, not just because there are no longer folk around him. His psychology gathers around us and him in a series of hints and glimpses, so that when the uncanny seeps into the tale we can't be sure where it began. It involves social observation too, and I'd call it allegorical. Let me not neglect to say that I'd have given quite a lot to have come up with the life raft image Gary has.

In recent years, I've enjoyed resurrecting or at least referring to occultists who figure in earlier work of mine, and sometimes transcribing more of their thoughts. The earliest is Roland Franklyn, and Matthew M. Bartlett's "We Pass from View" recalls him in much more than its title. The bookshop setting and the desperate summons echo tales of mine, as do smaller subtler details, but Bartlett's brilliance with imagery and language brings many a fresh observation—ways to make us look again at the familiar, as I try to do myself. The story itself is a thoroughly witty and wittily thorough variation on its source, with room for some fine nightmares of its own.

At first sight, when he was one of the rising generation of writers in our field, I knew Gary Fry had potential. If I say his talent isn't beyond words, that's because for him it's the words that count, and his accumulated skill in wielding them—no passing phase. This time it's showcased in "Meeting the Master." If even one word were blacked out, the effect of his prose would be compromised, and you won't think any line of his is mere cold print—let alone consisting of dead letters—by the time you reach the end of the line. In the best way, he belongs to the old school of our field, though he seldom has recourse to ancient images. Like many of our contributors, he has my obsession with language in the bag. (I certainly wouldn't have expected any of them to call first to make sure they'd caught the influence, and I can see they've had no end of fun.) Gary is adept at drawing in the reader, and he can make you see with the refreshed eye of childhood. At the end, his contribution becomes a kind of bedtime story, with a coda just waiting to happen, but perhaps not one you'd want to recall in the dark, especially when you're going under. I don't mind admitting he had me looking out some of my tales to make sure I spotted the pattern in his, but as far as I can tell after digging deep there's no missed connection, and I have the impression I'm out of the woods. I don't think I'm getting it wrong, and so I'll ignore the little voice that suggests a second sight would show how much more Gary has been playing the game with me. I was wrapped up in his narrative until the book was laid down, and the last thing I'd say is that it has no story in it. Anyway, think yourself lucky I've come to the end of this paragraph.

Kristi DeMeester's "Saints in Gold" has an oppressive autobiographical feel. Some of the details uncannily suggest the author could have been present at my childhood—details such as the sense of being trapped in religion like amber (in gold). Like so many of the stories in our book, it offers images that seize my mind, not entirely without envy: the room slipping out of its skin . . . The narrator drops a hint of his unreliability early on, but this only intensifies the disquiet the tale accumulates. In an essay Kristi DeMeester writes that "I am only writing the things I've kept buried for so long, pulling them up from the dark places of my childhood and examining the truth of them." No wonder the story feels so authentically personal and yet, at least in my experience, universal.

I once had a go at writing an Arabian tale, when I was all of fifteen and hadn't even travelled far in England. I suppose it was my bid to carry on the tradition of "The Nameless City," but in writing his story I'm sure Lovecraft had done more research, and certainly had a more developed imagination. Can that adolescent trifle of mine have somehow generated Cody Goodfellow's "This Last Night in Sodom"? I once planned a tale involving a team from Brichester University too, but never did. Goodfellow puts one together, along with much else of mine: the Lovecraftian influence, atheism versus Christianity, the foregrounding of the erotic, the unreliability of language, the protagonist whose introversion gradually turns paranoid, and—well, let me not identify the monster in case you've yet to read his tale. I'm astonished by how much he finds to develop in that old idea of mine and makes his own, and by gum, he gets graphic.

Kaaron Warren's "The Whither" reminds me of the terseness I discovered more than forty years ago, in stories such as "Call First," a knack I seem subsequently to have mislaid. She deftly sketches scene and character and situation in a way I'd like to rediscover, and there isn't a wasted word in her build-up of unease, starting with the resonant title. Her urban spectre may be an unrecorded species, but it has the strength of a legend.

In "Uncanny Valley" Jeffrey Thomas impressively elaborates on an old story of mine. He keeps catching me, the reader, off guard and makes me look again if not perform a productive double take. The sense of dread the story gathers is built up with splendid subtlety, and some of his images border on the subliminal. Daylight brings no relief, merely illuminating the uncanny and yet leaving it mysterious—the perfect end, in my view.

Lynda E. Rucker's "The Dublin Horror" celebrates an aspect of that city (which swarms with bookshops, and where a taxi driver who once picked me up at the airport talked learnedly about James Joyce throughout the drive) before homing in on the local breed of oppressive Catholicism (often exported to England, where I remember it all too well). Alas, her Dublin bookshop invokes the baleful influence of a writer not, I hope, too much like me. His words exert uncanny power, but then so do Lynda's, especially when she gradually but relentlessly pulls the narrative from under us, to end in poignant terror.

Thana Niveau begins "The Sixth Floor" with a barrage of references that should make the reader smile—they did me—before the gathering details grow ominous. Not for by any means the first time in this book, I have the fancy that I've used another writer to develop a story lurking somewhere in my mind. I may mention that we and our spouses have stayed in the same wretched hotels, which helps explain why the accommodation in her tale feels unsettlingly familiar. The tale itself is far from familiar, and withholds the source of its accumulated dread almost to the nightmare end. Bravo for using a local landmark in quite a different way from how I once did.

Christopher Slatsky takes us to revisit a sylvan setting in "The Carcass of the Lion," and anyone familiar with the location may well suspect anything that lives there. Slatsky's sense of a haunted forest recalls mine but is all his own, swarming with images that revive its mystery and seed it with new otherworldly life. The novel I set there used Lovecraft as to some extent a template but attempted to reach back through him to works he admired. While I won't claim to have proved myself worthy of the tradition, Slatsky is, and attains awe.

How did Kurt Vonnegut get in here? Orrin Grey's "The Granfalloon" invites him or at any rate brings in his influence. I've read his work avidly ever since I encountered *The Sirens of Titan*, as the finger-marked grubbiness of my copy of the first British paperback attests. Grey wittily introduces a Vonnegut theme to a number of mine, but knowing this by no means lessens the dread Grey gradually builds. His title has more than one meaning, and its ultimate significance brings cosmic fear.

Adam L. G. Nevill first came to my elated notice when I was co-editing *Gathering the Bones* with Dennis Etchison and Jack Dann. I used his remarkable tale "Mother's Milk," and we've been friends ever since, but I would never have expected him to repay my enthusiasm with such a tribute as "Little Black Lamb." His roots are in the great tradition of our field, and if he regards my stuff as part of that, I couldn't be happier. Like so much of this book, though, he invents a new dread, or perhaps finds it in the depths of our shared consciousness. He closes the volume on a note of hideous horror that is equally the product of restraint and suggestiveness—one of his great talents, and occasionally mine, I hope.

If this tale and the rest of the contents suggest I've shared a little of my inky self with the contributors, my career has been worthwhile. Or perhaps Roland Franklyn was right all along in *We Pass from View*. Perhaps everyone involved in this book, including me, is a facet of an infinite self.

Undertow Publications:
An Interview with Michael Kelly

Daniel Pietersen

The short story, that quick stab from the shadows, has always been a fertile breeding ground for weird fiction. However, if the short story is a single cut into our assumed reality, then what constitutes the whirl of blades that slices it into pieces? From the seminal *Weird Tales* through to the modern clutch of journals that Ashley Dioses covered in a recent article for this publication, there has been no way to lose yourself in a whirl of invention quite like a well-curated anthology, and there is no anthology quite as well curated as Undertow Publications' *Year's Best Weird Fiction*.

Undertow have taken a simple conceit, gathering exemplars of the weird tale from the past year's crop of publications into a single volume, and adding a hint of spice to the mix: a guest editor who has the final say as to which stories are included. Not only does this ensure that the series doesn't simply reflect the preferences of Michael Kelly, editor-in-chief of Undertow, but it allows each book to develop its own distinct character, just as each guest editor is a distinct character.

I spoke to Michael about Undertow and the *Year's Best Weird Fiction* series specifically. Our discussion is presented below, with divergences into thoughts on each of the four volumes published in the series so far.

DP: Can you first give me a little background on yourself, Michael? How you got into weird fiction and eventually came to publishing it. Are there any key titles or authors for you and your interest in the genre?

MK: I've always been an avid reader, from a very young age. I started out reading science fiction and fantasy—the usual suspects Asimov, Philip K. Dick, Jack L. Chalker, Tolkien, Ray Bradbury, Octavia Butler, Tiptree, Le Guin—then gravitated to horror, where

I discovered Clive Barker, Shirley Jackson, Charles Beaumont, Stephen King, Vernon Lee, etc. My interest then, as it is now, was short fiction. It's all I publish. Early on I devoured the anthologies of Judith Merrill, then Terry Carr, and as I started to read more horror I discovered Machen, Blackwood, Ligotti, Lovecraft, du Maurier, and many others. That led to Kafka, Bruno Schulz, and Alfred Kubin. But the short form fascinated me. Collections and anthologies, magazines and periodicals, were my "go to."

These three books, more than any others, I suspect, shaped the press:

Great Tales of Terror and the Supernatural, edited by Phyllis Wagner and Herbert Wise
The Howling Man by Charles Beaumont
The Dark Descent, edited by David G. Hartwell

These were the formative books that knocked me on my ass and proved that weird fiction, horror fiction, genre work, was literate, vital, and important.

DP: I first became aware of Undertow through the *Shadows & Tall Trees* collections, but your library extends from those to single-author collections of short stories and the *Year's Best Weird Fiction* series, which we'll delve into later. Can you give me a brief history of Undertow as a publishing entity?

MK: I love short fiction. It's mostly what I read. And mostly what I wrote—back when I used to write. I love the economy of the short form. It's a precise, compact, and exacting form. I dabbled in the short form and also co-wrote a novel. Along with the anthologies I used to read, I also read a number of small-press magazines. This was back when I was gravitating toward weird fiction and the horror genre, and back when desktop publishing was taking off and zines were basically put together and printed and folded at the local Kinko's or print shop. "Lit rags" is my affectionate term for these publications. Those zines had personality. I read *Palace Corbie, Grue, Cemetery Dance, Thin Ice, Eldritch Tales, The Horror Show, The Blue Lady, Crossroads, Gathering Darkness, Lore, Nasty Piece of Work, Sackcloth & Ashes,* and many more. I even placed stories in a number of zines.

Even as I voraciously read all the zines and anthologies I could, I always felt that there was a branch of the genre that wasn't being completely fulfilled, specifically the literate weird story or supernatural ghost story. Sure, there were examples of it, but too often, I felt that horror and weird fiction was being portrayed or viewed as a pejorative. Indeed, much of it deserved to be thoroughly disregarded and ridiculed.

Initially, I simply wanted to publish an anthology of subtle weird fiction that featured exceptional writing. So in 2008–09 I conceived *Apparitions* and invited some writers to contribute. It was very well received and earned a Shirley Jackson nomination, with a few stories reprinted in various "best of" anthologies. Emboldened, I started my own "lit rag"—*Shadows & Tall Trees*. It was a small, slim journal with clean design. At first it featured nonfiction, too. After five issues, I moved it to anthology size and dropped the nonfiction. Much to my delight, *Shadows & Tall Trees* has also struck a chord with readers. Of course, I've now branched off into single-author collections and also do the annual *Year's Best Weird Fiction*.

DP: Did you plan for it to turn into what it is today?

MK: No, not really. I really, truly only wanted to do that first anthology. To get that out of my system. To put something out there and say "Hey, let's have more of this stuff!" I was going to do the book, then get back to writing. But, as it turns out, I kept publishing more, and the writing has taken a back seat. Honestly, I'm still not sure I know what I'm doing. I'm publishing stuff I like, and just hoping others like it enough so that I can keep doing it. In many ways, the press is still evolving, still growing. I am, to be honest, crap at the business side. But I'm learning. I love doing it, though, despite all the headaches involved. It's a tremendous amount of work. *Year's Best Weird Fiction* alone eats up an enormous amount of time. I'd love to be able to do it full-time.

Year's Best Weird Fiction: Volume One

Volume One, predictably, sets the format for future volumes to follow: a foreword by Kelly, discussing the concept of "the weird" as well as thanking contributors and supporters, followed by an introduction by the guest editor, in this case Laird Barron. Barron, a fine author of weird tales in himself, cuts directly to the conundrum that lies at the heart of these anthologies when he says, "There are too many shades of weird, too many striations, and too many layers in the fossil record of this particular literary vein to proclaim 'greatest' or 'best' with any authority." Yet it is this admission that also supports the choice to use guest editors rather than a single, overarching voice: each volume is a qualified best-of, based on the tastes and admitted biases of the guest editor.

Although the collection of twenty-two stories is almost universally excellent, there are a handful that stand out for me, acting as my own personal guest editor, and feel worthy of special comment. Jeffrey Thomas's "In Limbo" is one of those wonderful, fallen-through-the-cracks tales that, through the protagonist's spiritual thinness turning into a breach in reality, exemplifies the thread of exile that runs through weird fiction. "Like Feather, Like Bone" by Kristi DeMeester is as delicate as the avian bones that crackle under the skin of her characters, whereas Jeff VanderMeer's "No Breather in the World But Thee" is a dense, Gothic distillation of some corrupted, Gormenghastian nightmare.

DP: What do you have in the Undertow pipeline for the coming months/years?

MK: Well, 2018 is shaping up to be a great year. In April, I will be releasing *All the Fabulous Beasts,* the debut short story collection from acclaimed British writer Priya Sharma. Priya is a natural and gifted storyteller, and I am extremely fortunate to have snagged publication rights for her first book. It's an amazing collection. There's always the October release of the *Year's Best Weird Fiction,* and this year will see Volume 5, guest-edited by the redoubtable Robert Shearman. I can't believe it'll be five volumes already. Also, in October, I'll be publishing Simon Strantzas's latest collection, *Nothing Is Everything.* I'm biased, to be sure, but I think this is Simon's finest work to date. He told me that it's an Undertow book, that he really couldn't envision it at another press. I agree. When folks ask me what I publish, I'll point them to this book. Simon's and Priya's books really epitomize what I'm all about. I do hope people like them. Those three books will compromise my annual subscription.

I generally offer four books in my subscription packages, but the fourth book I'm publishing this year is a bit of an outlier— the first volume of *The Silent Garden,* edited by the Silent Garden Collective, an anonymous group of writers, editors, and scholars. It's a cooperative venture, and I'm publishing the book on their behalf. It'll strictly be a hardcover edition, no trade or ebook versions. It looks extremely promising and should be out in July. *The Silent Garden* is a peer-reviewed journal of esoteric fabulism, edited and curated by the Silent Garden Collective, a professional group of editors, writers, and scholars interested in exploring those liminal borderlands where darkness bends.

The Collective's aim is to provide an annual journal of exceptional writing and art focused on horror and the numinous, the fabulist, the uncanny, the weird, the gnostic, the avant-garde, the esoteric, and the dark interstices of the known and unknown world.

Each volume of *The Silent Garden* will feature original, translated, and reprint fiction and nonfiction, including film and book reviews, essays, opinion and commentary, as well as poetry and art.

All contributions to the journal are peer-reviewed and vetted by the Silent Garden Collective. As well, the Collective is ever-changing and organic. Each volume will be helmed by a different group. Hence the anonymous nature.

Year's Best Weird Fiction: Volume Two

Guest editor Kathe Koja uses her introduction to talk about our human ability to detect the strange, to sense a break from the expected, as a further sense beyond the accepted blend of sight, sound, touch, taste, smell, and the more ephemeral sense of self. Extending from this thought is the idea that if a clash between our sense of apparent and actual motion causes nausea, then can the weird be caused by a shearing of expected reality and experienced reality?

This is reflected in some of the standout stories in the collection. In Siobhan Carroll's "Wendigo Nights," self and time collapse into sparkling parts as fractured as the ice underneath the story's Arctic base setting. In "Observations about Eggs from the Man Sitting Next to Me on a Flight from Chicago, Illinois to Cedar Rapids, Iowa," Carmen Maria Machado make us reassess our assumptions about the weird tale itself, using this moment of dislocation to turn banalities into tensions. A more patently weird tale, although weird in the sense of distorted human relations, Charles Wilkinson's "Hidden in the Alphabet" manages to elevate the relatively innocuous power of the optician, so often commanding those of us who see differently to challenge and explain our perception of the ordered real, to haunting levels of vengeance even as, in retrospect, the finale is spelled out in crystal clarity.

DP: I'd like to draw out one of the most striking elements of Undertow's work beyond the writing itself; the startling cover artwork. In a world where "horror" works often have a fairly horrible aesthetic, Undertow's editions are, quite frankly, beautiful. This is obviously an important part of the work of a publisher for you, but can you tell me more about how you select artwork for each book?

MK: Thanks so much for the kind words. Much of the credit for the look and feel of the books belongs to Vince Haig, Art Director, and good egg. Each book's specific aesthetic is very important to me. I've always believed you should judge a book by its cover. If I'm going to publish, I want it to look good.

For the trade and ebook editions I generally scout about for an existing piece of art that I really like, that I think fits the theme of the book. This is done with careful consideration and input from the author. Obviously, I don't want them unhappy with their cover. I've seen so many authors displeased with their book covers. One of the advantages of working with an independent press is that decisions and choices are cooperative and collaborative in nature. One hopes. I want my authors happy and involved.

For the hardcovers, which have a distinctive black and white theme, I use my secret weapon—Vince Haig. I commission Vince to illustrate the hardcovers. The exception being Priya Sharma's *All the Fabulous Beasts*. Jeffrey Alan Love had already done a great piece for Priya's story on Tor.com, so I licensed the art from Jeffrey.

DP: What made you want to use different artwork for the trade and hardback versions of each publication?

MK: The first hardback I did, the *Year's Best Weird Fiction,* Volume 3, shared the same cover as the trade edition. But moving forward I figured that the trade and hardback markets were two different beasts, so why not offer a different version? And why not aesthetically link all the hardcovers, design-wise, so they share a similar look and feel and theme? The Undertow hardcovers are easily distinguishable, I think. Economics also played a part in my decision. It costs a bit more to commission the separate cover. But I hoped folks would want to collect them. They haven't actually sold as much as I'd hoped.

Year's Best Weird Fiction: Volume Three

"Weird fiction is just another name for Horror fiction." This is the assertion that Simon Strantzas makes in his introduction to Volume 3 and it's a bold one, especially when a lot of time has been taken, both in this series and other works, to say exactly the opposite. I'm unsure whether I agree with the thought, but what I do agree with is Strantzas's belief that the core of a weird tale is when "terror flows from the world not being as it seems."

This intermingling of mode and genre can be seen in Nadia Bulkin's "Violet Is the Colour of Your Energy," a blend of horror, weird, and science fiction that bleed into one another like the radioactive smearing of color that infects both the characters and the narrative itself. In the eerie post-apocalyptic Cambridge of Marian Womack's "Orange Dogs," where luxuries such as marmalade are more valuable than gold, this blending occurs again— a speculative horror that drops us into a world both recognizable and utterly alien. Reggie Oliver takes a very British banality, the colorless life of decrepit seaside towns, and squeezes a subtle, slow-moving horror from it in "The Rooms Are High."

DP: For me, Undertow's books are objects that demand to be held in the hand and admired, something that I think digital publishing, for all its benefits, misses out on. What are your thoughts on the physical-versus-digital elements of publishing?

MK: I'm a tactile person. I love a physical book: the feel; the smell; the heft. What people find odd about me, I've heard, is that I am not a collector. I don't go out of my way to acquire books to keep, though I do keep several hundred. Most of the books I buy and read eventually get recycled or donated, occasionally pulped (in which case I am doing the reading public a favor). While I do prefer reading a printed book, I have no qualms about ebooks. I'll happily read them. And will continue to offer ebooks. In fact, most of my sales, perhaps surprisingly, now come from ebooks. That's been a gradual shift. And perhaps it's a generational shift. Either way, long live the printed word!

DP: Let's talk a bit about your *Year's Best Weird Fiction* series, which is the focus of this piece. Can you give me a bit of background on where the idea for this series came from?

MK: Well, there seemed to be a renewed interest in weird fiction, though, truthfully, I believe the interest was always there. We were just calling it something else. Slipstream? Horror? My friend Scott Nicolay championed what he called the "Weird Renaissance." While I don't particularly like that term—"renaissance" is a bit of a loaded term, I think—I applaud his enthusiasm and feel he's on the right track. There's a moment happening now in weird fiction that feels inspiring and important. And, frankly, with all the other "Best Of" anthologies flooding the market, I couldn't fathom why there was no distinct, separate book for weird fiction. I couldn't believe no one was doing one. I wanted one. And it seemed no one else wanted to do one, so I did. I funded the first volume via a crowd-funding campaign. And now Robert Shearman and I are finalizing Volume 5. Five volumes. Wow. I can hardly believe we've made it this far.

DP: Obviously there are a large number of weird fiction collections out there, and the number seems to be growing daily, but it strikes me that *YBWF* has two key selling points: the consistently excellent level of content and, perhaps most importantly, the concept of a guest editor for each volume with yourself as "series coordinator." Where did this idea come from and how do you select guest editors?

MK: I've always liked the idea of a guest editor. Houghton Mifflin employs them for their *Best American Mystery Stories* series, with Otto Penzler as Series Editor, and also their *Best American*

Science Fiction and Fantasy series, with John Joseph Adams as Series Editor (though my series predates the Adams). It's a way to keep the series fresh and to also show the breadth of weird fiction. I always get flak for mentioning this, but it's true—"Best Ofs" with a single editor often rely on a small group of the same writers year in and year out. You can simply look at the various table of contents of some recent volumes to verify this. This isn't necessarily a bad thing. It's the editor's taste, after all. And we have some fine editors helming these books. But in terms of optics, perception, and overall flavor and voice of the books, I feel I'm often getting the same book each year.

I try to choose a guest editor who will bring a certain passionate and singular sensibility to the series. And I try to choose someone to bring an array of voices and tastes to the position. I usually have a sense of the guest editor's taste beforehand, and I try to play off the previous year's editor, in that regard.

DP: What's the process for "harvesting" stories for the collections? Do you actively search for relevant work or rely on submissions? You often mention in your forewords that you have issues with some publishers responding to requests. Is this still an issue?

MK: I do actively solicit submissions, and I do read far and wide. I'll read all the genre publications and websites, plus I tend to read all the "lit" journals that also might have some weird stuff, like *Conjunctions,* the *New Yorker, Black Clock, Granta, Phantom Drift,* etc. I cast a wide net. Anthologies, collections, magazines, journals, websites. I'm always reading. And I keep my ear close to the ground, trying to find out what people are reading and talking about. I think our series has the most stories in it that come from non-genre sources.

I will ask publishers or editors to send me a PDF, or other electronic file, of their book or journal. After some time, I will check my list, and if they haven't responded I will send a polite follow-up email. That's it, though. I won't ask again. I haven't time to keep following up and hounding people. You'd be surprised how many do not respond. Or respond well after my deadline.

Year's Best Weird Fiction: Volume Four

In her introduction to the fourth, and currently most recent, volume of this series, Helen Marshall talks about apocalypse and its original meaning as an uncovering or unveiling. This is pivotal to horror, specifically weird horror, in showing us either how the world could change or, sometimes more horrifically, how it has changed without us even realizing it. Apocalyptic change, revelatory change is a liminal zone that allows expectations to be confounded and assumptions to be corroded.

Katie Knoll's "Red," a haunting meditation on female puberty and the otherness it creates, uses this apocalypse, the uncovering of female potential, to great effect. Another form of uncovering, peeling away layers of lie and self-deception, sits at the heart of "A Heavy Devotion" by Daisy Johnson. The revelation of a world-behind, a different layer of reality, is explicit in "Breakdown" by Gary Budden, a wonderfully tight vignette.

DP: Can you talk about the responsibilities of the guest editor and yourself when it comes to story selection?

I'll do the bulk of the reading. The guest editors generally do a lot of reading on their own. There have been stories that we've taken that I didn't even see during my reading. So that's another benefit of a guest editor. Generally, over the course of the year, I will send sixty to eighty stories total to my guest editor. I try to send a mix of stories that I like and that I think the guest editor might like. From there, they have to choose about 100,000 words of fiction. I know there are some "Year's Bests" doing twice that amount of fiction, but that's ridiculous, quite frankly. Really? They are all the best? They are clearly not. They are filling a quota.

While the fiction I send over to the guest editor has been filtered through my lens, I want to emphasize that ALL the final selections for the book are from the guest editor. It's their book. Once the guest editor has chosen their stories I ask them to put them in the order they'd like, and to also write an introduction to the volume. And that's the extent of their duties. Sounds easy, but it's not. It's a lot of reading, and a lot of agonizing over stories.

DP: Does the order of the stories mean a lot to you? I feel that the collections often nicely balance short and long, frightening and unsettling stories well.

MK: It's very important. And very hard to get right. Lots of folks will read out of order, anyway. The guest editor, having read all my curated selections, will be tasked with finding the right order. Often, without even realizing it, the stories seem to suggest a certain order. It's magic!

DP: You have published four volumes to date. What have you learned over the publication of these four volumes, either about creating the collections themselves or the wider market for weird fiction collections?

MK: Wow, tough question. I'm still learning. As I write this we are finalizing Volume 5. I've learned that it is an awful lot of work, as I knew it would be. Anthologies, in general, have a lot of moving parts. This one more so, given that it has a guest editor, and that the reading never ends. I estimate I read between 2500 and 2800 stories any given year. I've learned that writers shouldn't give away their rights—that big publishing houses are a pain to deal with in terms of rights, permissions, and rates—and that, for the most part, readers seem to appreciate what I am doing.

In terms of the market for weird fiction, it seems to be growing. It's showing up in venues like *Granta* and *The New Yorker,* even if those venues don't call it weird fiction. And it's being regularly review in places like the *New York Times* and *Publishers Weekly,* and more. It's an exciting time.

DP: This is probably a hard question to answer, but do you have any particular favorite tales from the collections? There are certainly ones that stand out for me. Equally, are there any stories you've found after the fact that you wish could have been included?

MK: Sometimes a story just hits you, you know. Hits all the buttons. For me, that story was "The Earth and Everything Under," by K. M. Ferebee, which appeared in Volume 2, guest edited by Kathe Koja. Love that story. To me, it's a standout. The great thing is, everyone has a different favorite.

DP: What does the future hold for *YBWF*? How far in advance do you plan the guest editors for future volumes? Will there be a Decade's Best Weird Fiction?

MK: Guest editors are usually selected about 6 months to a year in advance. However, while I've talked to a few possible editors for volume 6, nothing is yet officially signed. I hope to keep doing this. My original plan was to do 5 volumes and reevaluate. I'm at the point where the amount of time and energy to continue the series is dwindling. The rest of my catalogue takes up a significant amount of time, as does my day job. Something will likely have to give. Or I need to hire some help. To be perfectly honest, what the series needs more than anything else is sales. Unfortunately, sales haven't lived up to my expectations. But I never got into this to make money. I always believed that if I put out a good product that it would sell. I still believe that.

With Volume 5 now in its planning stages, and Robert Shearman on board as guest editor, there is even more incentive to pick up a couple of copies of this "good product." *The Year's Best Weird Fiction,* as well as the rest of Undertow's catalogue, can be ordered through its website; http://www.undertowbooks.com/.

Ghosts and Critics Hand in Hand

Jim Rockhill

SCOTT BREWSTER and LUKE THURSTON, ed. *The Routledge Handbook to the Ghost Story*. New York: Routledge, 2018. xviii, 487 pp. $240.00 hc, $54.95 ebook. ISBN: 978-1-138-18476-3.

At nearly 500 closely packed pages, offering 48 essays divided into 6 sections detailing how the ghost story's early development out of the Gothic and Romantic novel was shaped by its literary and social milieux as well as philosophical, aesthetic, and scientific debates ("Ghostly Origins"); studies focusing on a few key practitioners of the form ("Vital Spirits"); as well as explorations of how the form developed in different nations ("Haunted Nations"); how and where authors have chosen to reveal their manifestations from landscapes, modes of transport, tourism, the peculiar atmosphere of battlefields, haunted houses, and children's literature ("Haunting Sites"); how ghost stories have been treated and reshaped for the stage, early visual and mechanical media, radio, film, television, and the Internet ("Ghosts on Screen and Stage"); how writers of ghostly fiction have responded to issues of aversion, animals, feminism, sexual orientation, the challenges of postmodern culture, and a post-colonial world ("Ghosts in Theory"); and a coda on "Ghosts and the Ethics of Literature," this ambitious volume

> sets out to survey and significantly extend a new field of criticism which has been taking shape over recent years, centering on the ghost story and bringing together a vast range of interpretive methods and theoretical perspectives. The main task of the volume is to properly situate the genre within historical and contemporary literary cultures across the globe, and to explore its significance within wider literary contexts as well as those of the supernatural. The Handbook offers the most significant contribution to this new critical field to date, assembling some of its leading scholars to examine the key contexts and issues required for understanding the emergence and development of the ghost story.

It promises and delivers a fascinating and insightful read, though the extent to which it fully lives up to that promise occasionally falters due to the aforementioned issue with its declared scope and in how some of the scholars apply "key contexts and issues" to their chosen material.

The statements quoted appear on page 3 of the introduction, on the rear cover, and on the publisher's webpage; thus, there should be little question about the work's scope, yet the table of contents suggest a narrower focus, which is confirmed within a few pages. The section on "Vital Spirits" presents seven men and three women, all of them writing in English, and the majority of them writing in England. For a volume that seeks to address "historical and contemporary literary cultures across the globe" not to examine in depth a single author writing in other areas of Europe, when each of these nations offers rich supernatural traditions of their own, presents a serious paradox.

This is compounded when the "Haunted Nations" section that follows devotes seven separate essays to Anglophone ghost stories written in England, Scotland, Wales, America, English-language Canada, Australia, and New Zealand, but only five to an eclectic selection of other nations: the Caribbean, Latin America, South Africa, India, and China; nor do all the authors covered in even those chapters write outside the English language. If this seems to represent not the entire world but merely Britain, its colonies and outposts at their most expansive, the true scope of the book becomes clear during the long, excellent introduction, during which the editors declare Britain as "what might complacently be deemed the 'home' of the ghost story" amid repeated references to the individual essays in their book in terms of how they reflect the development to and from the Victorian ghost story. Those wishing to read about the contributions of de Maupassant, Pushkin, or other writers of Continental ghost stories will, therefore, be disappointed by a book that views the form as primarily a British construct, impinging upon, coming into conflict with, or enriched by other cultural traditions and modes of communication. Aside from the statement that "many Irish writers have played a prominent part in the ghost story tradition," several Irish writers receive attention in chapters throughout the book without a separate chapter on their nation: "to assimilate them into a British context is problematic" due to "conflicting cultural, political, linguistic, and religious allegiances engendered by colonial history," even though similar conflicts arising from the ferment of indigenous beliefs vs. European religion, mythology vs. rationalism, acquiescence or assimilation vs. dissent, and the quest for a national identity that synthesized indigenous and colonial elements of a shared heritage (whether wrongs perpetrated by colonists were recognized as such) not only did not disqualify other "Haunted Nations" from discussion in Section 3, but were to be considered elements that lent them distinction.

All the essays in "Ghostly Origins" are excellent, taking into account their focus on British literature toward and beyond the Victorian ghost story. Of especial note are Jarlath Killeen's witty probing of the "culture clash between the kind of ghost story phantoms being investigated by the Society of Psychical Research and those traditionally associated with the Gothic" in "Oscar Wilde in the Fourth Dimension" and Brittany Roberts's "Ghost Stories and Sensation Fiction," concerned with the blurring of lines distinguishing supernatural fiction from the more melodramatic elements of fiction written by Wilkie Collins, Le Fanu, and Mary Elizabeth Braddon ostensibly taking place in a real world filled with canny villains, deadly *femmes fatales,* complex cabals, doughty detectives, and families imperiled by financial liability, mental illness, and the threat of shame or death.

It might at first seem odd to see Sir Arthur Conan Doyle and the now relatively unknown Margaret Oliphant among the elite group receiving chapters of their own, when Edgar Allan Poe, Ambrose Bierce, Fritz Leiber, and Ramsey Campbell are absent, among many others who have contributed significantly to reshaping the English-language ghost story to reflect contemporary concerns while retaining aesthetic appeal. Nonetheless, and given the centripetal focus upon the Victorians, Elizabeth McCarthy's "Haunting Memories: Death, Mourning, and Memory in the Ghost Stories of Margaret Oliphant" and Kevin Mills's "Conan Doyle's Sceptical Reader: Ghost Stories, Science and Spiritualism" earn their place in this volume, as does Claire Wood's "Playful Spirits: Charles Dickens and the Ghost Story," through the lucidity of their prose and the skill with which these scholars demonstrate how authors responded to and helped reshape current attitudes about life, death, and morality; created works of enduring merit while responding to the fickle demands of the marketplace; and provided models for future writers to develop (or demolish). McCarthy's essay is particularly fine in establishing the chronology and integrity of her prolific author's career and the way her few, carefully written ghost stories deal with "a tension between earthly and divine parentage" that acknowledges the necessity for "a space for meditations on bereavement outside of a strictly Christian perspective" or the disputed comforts of Spiritualism. "Oliphant's 'work of mourning' in her ghost stories and other writing, doesn't mean separation but connection; the restoration of human ties despite death's severing of physical ones."

The canonical status conferred upon Joseph Sheridan Le Fanu, Algernon Blackwood, M. R. James, and Henry James in this volume should surprise no one familiar with the history of supernatural literature and the dreadful fascination these authors continue to elicit from readers. Each of the essays accorded them is excellent, but two call for special comment. Alison Milbank navigates through the polyvalent nature of Le Fanu's supernatural fiction with rare insight and concision, pointing out the different forms of duality within the work, the layering of narrators and time periods, the metaphysical dimension of the author's spiritual terrors that effects a "congruence of symbolic and physical haunting," the complex use to which the author uses animals, the iconography that lends depths to the sordid adventure of "Schalken the Painter," the author's "ability to suggest in his haunting meanings beyond what is overtly stated," and a witty description of the many interpretations of "Carmilla" in which "the supernatural is often actually ignored as "overdetermined decodings." S. T. Joshi's essay is equally acute, not only in outlining the force of Blackwood's focus on Nature and the subtlety of his methods, but also in choosing the perfect quotation to capture the essence of each work discussed.

The inclusion of Oliver Tearle's "Vernon Lee," Emily Colt's "'A Roaring and Discontinuous Universe': Edith Wharton's Modern Haunting," and Timothy Jones's "'German Has a Word for the Total Effect': Robert Aickman" is equally welcome. If the exalted position accorded these authors within this volume might seem paradoxical to some considering the exclusion of so many other candidates, each of these authors has a unique way of exhibiting how society and the individual interact, how the individual's responses to external stimuli are shaped by memory, and how those interactions in turn affect the individual's response to perceived impingements from the spiritual plane. Aickman, like Dickens, is just as important as an editor as he is as a writer of ghostly fiction, though the quality and influence of his own fiction did not begin to be fully recognized until the beginning of the present century.

Moving on to "Haunted Nations," the absence of Edgar Allan Poe, Ambrose Bierce, and Fritz Leiber from the list of "Vital Spirits" is compounded by the narrowness of focus displayed by Jeffrey Andrew Weinstock's essay on "The American Ghost Story." Aside from a very fine discussion in tandem of Henry James's *The Turn of the Screw* and Shirley Jackson's *The Haunting of Hill House* in terms of their rejection of "the principles of Enlightenment rationalism that presumes individuals to be able to draw reasonable conclusions based on empirical data" and "call into question the extent to which human beings can know their own motivations and trust their senses," the only contexts Weinstock considers proper for the discussion of ghost stories in American literature appear to be the "connection between terror and *terroir*"; the "sour ground" created by "sacred space bearing the traces of historical injustice" and other forms of disenfranchisement extending from indigenous cultures to imported African slaves and women; the creation of formational myths in Washington Irving and Nathaniel Hawthorne; and the consolatory ghosts associated with the Spiritualist movement. Poe, Stephen King, and Mark Danielewski appear but briefly in this essay; Bierce once; the likes of Fritz Leiber, Russell Kirk, Richard Matheson (whose work is not even discussed in the chapters about film and television), and others not at all. It is not that Toni Morrison, Charlotte Perkins Gilman, and the others discussed here and elsewhere in the book do not deserve the attention they receive—they most assuredly do—but that there is much more to the American ghost story than is suggested within these pages. If one turns back to the essay on Blackwood with that author's description of New York as the "awful city, with its torrential, headlong life . . . something monstrous . . . a scab on the skin of the planet, brilliant with the hues of fever, moving all over with seeming microbes," one catches an early glimpse of the potential that Fritz Leiber captured in his Chicago Gothics: "Have you ever thought what a ghost of our times would look like, Miss Malick? Just picture it. A smoky composite face . . . It would grow out of the real world. It would reflect all the tangled, sordid, vicious things. All the loose ends." Unfortunately, this, along with the celebration of regional folklore by the likes of Manly Wade Wellman, the American Conservative reinterpretation of Victorian storytelling traditions in Russell Kirk, the threats peculiar to suburbia (so ably explored by Bernice M. Murphy in *The Suburban Gothic in American Popular Culture*), and several other strands in American supernatural fiction are absent from this discussion.

The essays in "Haunting Sites" and "Ghosts on Stage and Screen" are similarly fine once one accepts their almost exclusively British focus, as are those in "Ghosts in Theory," which, beginning with Pamela K. Gilbert's delightful "How Ghosts Became Disgusting," offer some of the most thought-provoking portions of the book.

Luke Thurston returns the reader's attention to Margaret Oliphant's "The Open Door," after a brief, related discussion of Henry James's "The Jolly Corner," to demonstrate how reading ghost stories offers "ways to voice a discontent with, or an implicit critique of, the ontological framework of 'everyday life.'" In the introduction, Thurston and his co-editor had referred to the "hugely influential binarism voiced by [George] Eliot in her 1859 bestseller *Adam Bede*," which posited that "only the traditional novel, with its weighty volume and narrative complexity, could make the reader's imagination work sufficiently hard to engage with the actual difficulty of real life," dismissing "other kinds of writing . . . suitable only for children." This essay, with the full title "Stories Not Like Any Others: Ghosts and the Ethics of Literature," forms the culmination of a book devoted to disputing such a narrow-minded assertion. That it succeeds is testimony to a book, which (despite faults of omission which the writer of this review fully expects to see addressed incrementally by scholars inspired by the example set by the editors and contributors to the present volume) lays down a firm foundation for future studies of the much-loved, though long-denigrated ghost story.

Spoken Art: Cadabra Record's "The Bungalow House" LP

Sam Cowan

THOMAS LIGOTTI. *The Bungalow House*. Read by Jon Padgett. Score by Chris Bozzone. Cadabra Records, 2018. 33⅓ rpm vinyl recording. $32.00.

I first encountered the work of Thomas Ligotti purely by chance. I was at a Borders bookstore in 2006, casually browsing the horror section. At that time I was reading mainly nonfiction, but I'd always look for certain authors when I went to book stores; I had been a fan of the *Weird Tales* writers since middle school and was on the lookout for new collections of their work. Borders had a couple of the Del Rey oversized paperback collections of associated H. P. Lovecraft stories, nothing I hadn't seen before, but just before the Lovecraft books there was another volume with no author name on the spine, just the title of the book—*The Shadow at the Bottom of the World*. Intrigued, I picked it up. The back cover mentioned Ligotti's writing as descending from Poe and Lovecraft. I decided to give it a shot.

The Shadow at the Bottom of the World is made up of fifteen stories taken from a number of Ligotti's earlier collections, with a new foreword by Ligotti and, I believe, the first appearance of his story "Purity." The first story in the book is "The Feast of Harlequin," probably Ligotti's best-known story and a direct nod to old HPL. It captivated me, and I devoured the book as quickly as I could.

Ligotti's work impacted me like few others. In middle school Lovecraft and Stephen King knocked me for a loop; during high school Clive Barker and Hunter S. Thompson made huge impressions on me; and now as an adult I finally had a similar experience. From that point forward I perceived the world in a slightly different way.

Of all the stories in that book, "The Bungalow House" was one of my favorites, along with "The Red Tower," "Teatro Grottesco," and "The Tsalal." I thoroughly enjoyed (if that is the right word) all the stories, but these four had special resonance for me.

A couple of years later I came across the vital Thomas Ligotti Online forum (http://ligotti.net) and immediately created an account. The site's creator, Jon Padgett, had recorded himself reading some of Ligotti's stories, and these readings were soon MP3s on my iPod. I listened to them a number of times, especially "The Bungalow House."

When I heard about Cadabra Records doing "The Bungalow House" as an LP, I was delighted to learn that Jon Padgett would be the reader. I thought of his YouTube reading of the story and wondered how they would compare. Having listened to both versions a few times lately, I believe they are both quite good despite their differences.

The Cadabra recording of "The Bungalow House" is simply fantastic. The pace of Padgett's reading is slightly faster than the YouTube version (54:27 versus 58:03), and I think on the whole it is more accessible. The YouTube recording is a little more idiosyncratic: Padgett's narrator has a creepier cadence, and the recording itself is of lower audio quality, although Ligotti scholar Matt Cardin's score matches the story nicely. In the Cadabra recording, the narrator sounds more like a regular person rather than a strange outsider, and Chris Bozzone's score appropriately moves from pleasant if slightly ominous to burbling and definitely ominous synth washes as the story progresses.

To put in another way, the YouTube recording reminds me of a band's demo tape: DIY all the way, a little rough around the edges but with passion to spare. The Cadabra recording is like that same band's second or third record: more confident, cleaner, and obviously produced with a real budget and an eye toward some commercial appeal. Some bands make this transition well and are able to hold on to the spark that initially inspired them to create, and that is the case here. I like both recordings, but it is the Cadabra version I will be revisiting most often.

The Cadabra release has been pressed on heavy swirled vinyl and is housed in a gorgeous gatefold jacket. The striking art by Jason Burnett meshes quite well with the overall ambience of the story. In addition to the record, the Cadabra release comes with a full-color 12-page booklet insert and a mini-poster. The booklet includes a new essay on "The Bungalow House" by Matt Cardin that I found fascinating and astute, and an insightful new interview with Ligotti himself. Both pieces helped give me a fuller context and better understanding of the story.

You can listen to the first five and a half minutes of the Cadabra release for yourself on Soundcloud (http://bit.ly/2FgDhfW), and I suggest that you do so soon, as the LP is limited to 500 copies.

If you are new to Ligotti, listen to the sample to get a sense of his writing style. If it appeals to you, welcome. "The Bungalow House" is a great entry point for his work and the dark wonders that lie ahead for you. Ligotti's first two collections are readily available as one volume through Penguin Classics, and much discussion of the man, his work, and associated topics can be found at Thomas Ligotti Online.

For Ligotti fans, this record is extremely attractive. Padgett's narration, Bozzone's score, and Burnett's art all come together in a way that gives us a unique peek at "a bungalow universe," and the included essay is an important new entry in the field of Ligotti studies.

Cadabra Records has done an outstanding job with everything here, both audio and visual, and I give "The Bungalow House" a solid A and my hearty recommendation.

Justified Obscurity

Ryne Davis

SEABURY QUINN. *The Complete Tales of Jules De Grandin: The Horror on the Links—Volume 1.* Ed. George A. Vanderburgh and Robert E. Weinberg. New York: Night Shade Books, 2017. 494 pp. $34.99 hc. ISBN: 978-1-59780-893-4.

A few years ago, I began building my book collection in earnest. This was triggered by the acquisition of several Arkham House titles, a publisher that had hitherto been a major blind spot for me. I bought the books slowly, focusing on *Weird Tales* authors of whose work I had read little or nothing. *Black Medicine* by Arthur J. Burks, *West India Lights* by Henry S. Whitehead, and several others were bought and quickly devoured. I kept an eye out for *The Phantom Fighter* by Seabury Quinn, a collection of his Jules de Grandin stories, but it remained elusive. I had previously read only one other story by Quinn, . . . *Roads,* which appeared in the January 1938 issue of *Weird Tales* and was later released by Arkham House as a stand-alone book. The story, a unique take on the origins of Christmas containing a protagonist seemingly stolen from a Robert E. Howard tale, was overall a very enjoyable read and made me more determined than ever to acquire *The Phantom Fighter*.

Then in the summer of last year I stumbled upon *The Horror on the Links,* the first of five volumes of the complete tales of Jules de Grandin by Night Shade Books. All ninety-three stories featuring the eccentric French detective are being collected in chronological order as they originally appeared in *Weird Tales* from 1925 to 1951. I purchased this attractive edition to familiarize myself with these stories and to find out if I really wanted to pay for the expensive Arkham House volume.

Night Shade has done an admirable job on the book itself: a quality trade hardcover with fantastic dust jacket art by Donato Giancola. The wrap-around illustration depicts de Grandin amidst a collage of horror tropes straight from the stories found within. An insightful introduction by editor George A. Vander-burgh and the late Robert E. Weinberg is also featured. At just under five hundred pages, *The Horror on the Links* is a formidable tome. Unfortunately, the quality of the contents within does not hold up to that of the book itself.

Before delving into the book's contents, a little background on Quinn's series. The Jules de Grandin stories were immensely popular with readers of *Weird Tales* in its heyday. After the first episode appeared in October 1925, letters poured in demanding more stories featuring de Grandin. Both Seabury Quinn and editor Farnsworth Wright were quick to oblige and began publishing de Grandin tales in many subsequent issues.

Seabury Quinn's series was not only popular with the readers of *Weird Tales* but also with many of the magazine's regular writers as well: Robert E. Howard, Manly Wade Wellman, Henry Kuttner, and Ray Bradbury all praised Quinn's tales. H. P. Lovecraft was apparently one of the few contemporary writers who did not think highly of them and often disparaged Quinn's work in his letters. The decades following the demise of "The Unique Magazine," however, saw Seabury Quinn slowly fade into obscurity, as the posthumous popularity of writers once overshadowed by his pen steadily rose.

Often set in the fictional town of Harrisonville, New Jersey, the stories chronicle the adventures of Dr. Jules de Grandin of the Paris Secret Police (among a slew of other accreditations) and Dr. Samuel Trowbridge, a local physician and the Dr. Watson to de Grandin's Holmes. The adversaries of our heroes are the usual horror fare: vampires, werewolves, mummies, and ghosts abound, although in a few instances, such as in "The Grinning Mummy" and "Creeping Shadows," the antagonists turn out to be malicious *foreigners* rather than anything supernatural.

Despite the multitude of adversaries our heroes face, each tale almost invariably follows the same basic formula. Something strange is afflicting one of Dr. Trowbridge's patients. De Grandin, intrigued by the unusual case, accompanies Trowbridge to the patient's residence, where the talented French sleuth discovers clues that suggest there is something evil afoot. De Grandin quickly learns the true cause of the problem but keeps this information to himself until the final confrontation with the antagonist, in which he invariably triumphs. In the final scene, de Grandin explains to Dr. Trowbridge how he figured it all out and saved the day, usually over a glass of brandy or cognac. This is the formula for nearly every one of the stories, which, in a five-hundred-page book containing twenty-three of these tales, becomes tiring. Perhaps, if read one story per month or so, as they were published in the original run of *Weird Tales,* this would not be as big of a problem.

Unfortunately, there are other defects to these stories. De Grandin's absurd expressions ("Nom d'un petit porc!") are frequent enough to become grating, and Dr. Trowbridge's incredulity at each new supernatural event is equally absurd given how many events of a similar nature he had previously experienced. In general, Quinn's writing is excessively purple, and there is a distinct lack of engrossing atmosphere.

Though authentic chills are few, these instances are memorable even if they are usually of the more visceral, gore-drenched variety. In "The House of Horror," de Grandin and Trowbridge unearth the gruesome results of a madman's experiments on young women who have lately gone missing. The climax of "The White Lady of the Orphanage" is also quite effective: Quinn reveals the monstrous things that had been taking place inside a small cottage with only a few hideous details. Sadly, the vast majority of the other tales are not of the same caliber.

Indeed, after the last story has been read, the prospect of acquiring the next book in the series is quite dim for me. I may end up buying *The Phantom Fighter* someday, though, if the price is right. But only as a matter of course as an Arkham House collector, not because of the quality of the contents.

"I'm Sorry. You Ate my Cat": A Fond Look at *Stranger Things 2*

Hank Wagner and Bev Vincent

Bev Vincent: So, *Stranger Things* is back with Season 2, or, as they have styled it, *Stranger Things 2*—as if a sequel, which is appropriate given it is more of an homage to classic feature films (like *Ghostbusters* and the *Alien* franchise) rather than to television. Hank and I took two different approaches to this new release. I watched all nine episodes in a one-day marathon session the day after they were released, whereas Hank spread them out over several days. For me, it was a totally immersive experience, akin to watching a (very long) feature film. Regardless of which way you choose, the experience is rewarding. Although the second season is bigger in many ways, I think it's safe to say that if you enjoyed the first season, you'll dig this one. It wasn't perfect—we'll get into that, I'm sure—but it was very, very good.

Hank Wagner: Bev, I have to cop to watching the first season a second time, marveling at how well it held up, then segueing immediately into ST2. Mom was right, I am ruining my eyes by watching too much television.

BV: And I'll admit to watching all of ST2 *again* while we were working on this article!

HW: So yes, *Stranger Things 2* is basically more of the same, only different. But that's definitely not a knock. ST2 expands on concepts developed in the first season, even while opening new avenues of exploration, for instance, briefly changing locales from Hawkins (which truly takes its place in the pantheon of classic haunted towns, like Castle Rock, Oxrun Station, and Arkham) to Chicago, where we meet Eleven's "sister." All the characters that made *Stranger Things* so special last time out are back, with some, like Will Bayers (Noah Schapp), who spent most of the first season trapped in the Upside Down, taking on larger roles, and others, like Mike Wheeler (Finn Wolfhard), stepping back a bit. There are also a handful of new characters, portrayed by Paul Reiser, Sean Astin, Sadie Sink, Dacre Montgomery, Linnea Berthelson, and Brett Gelman, among others. We'll cover them all in due time, but right now I feel compelled to discuss two of the coolest couples on television, Eleven and Jim Hopper, and Steve Harrington and Dustin Henderson.

BV: One of the neat things about this season is the way they've paired off characters who didn't have much to do with each other last time out. Hopper has a paternal relationship to Eleven that picks up from his Eggo drop-off at the end of Season 1, and he has good reason to be overprotective, but Eleven is a strong-willed character with awesome powers, so it's clear that it's only a matter of time before the rigid structure he has created to protect her and her isolation will lead to confrontation. "Don't be stupid" is one of the few rules he enforces, but both of them are guilty of breaking that one in different ways.

Steve is an interesting character. At the end of Season 1, I suspect viewers were irritated by the fact that Nancy picked him over Jonathan, but he's not a bad guy, and he demonstrates growth over the course of this season. He and Dustin come from different worlds, though. At that age, an older boy would have little use for someone even a year younger than he is, and by the same token Dustin only teams up with him because he feels abandoned by his other friends. And yet, when the danger starts to kick in, they become a hilarious duo. Almost a bromance, as they discuss dating and hair-styling tips while doing the *Stand by Me* walk along the train tracks.

Also this season, the world of Hawkins has expanded. Dustin has a mother, Lucas has a sister, Brenda has parents, Joyce has a boyfriend, and so on. They made the somewhat risky decision to open the season with a whole batch of people we've never seen before in a setting we aren't familiar with. Though intriguing—and we come to understand the general significance of that scene by its end because of the 008 tattoo, it takes a long time to pay off. And, when it does, it's in one of the most hotly debated episodes from the two seasons combined.

HW: I enjoyed Eleven's road trip of discovery midway through the season, where she met her mother, and found her lost comrade, the aforementioned 008 (Linnea Berthelson), the leader of a pack of young punks who are pursuing vengeance against former employees of Hawkins National Laboratory, the folks seeking to exploit Eleven, Eight, and the parallel dimension known as the Upside Down. While watching these episodes, I couldn't help but think of Stephen King in *Firestarter* and *The Tommyknockers* mode, two of his novels that featured the black ops organization known as The Shop. Also, departing from the show's tendency to lionize the '80s, I recalled the gang that the title character of *Chappie* fell in with during that movie. Eleven, the innocent, certainly undergoes a character arc similar to that of the robot who suddenly develops consciousness. But, returning to '80s, that made me think of Johnny Five from *Short Circuit,* even though that movie is two years in the future from *Stranger Things 2*.

BV: I liked Eleven's trip to find her mother, but I was less fond of the huge diversion to find her "sister." That felt more like *Orphan Black* than *Stranger Things*. Taking us away from what was happening in Hawkins for such a long stretch was risky, and I'm not sure it was wise. It may well be, though, that they are setting up things for Season 3 that required that bit of storytelling. Eleven (whose real name we now know) did some growing up and learned a few things about herself and her powers from this side-quest, and she did need them for the final confrontation, but that section felt disruptive to me.

On the other hand, I really liked what they did with some of the new characters. First you have Murray Bauman (Gelman), the former journalist turned private investigator, the prototypical conspiracy theory junkie who just happens to be right about some of his wacky theories. He comes off as smarmy and no one in authority listens to him, but they should. His scenes with Nancy and Jonathan are fantastic, double entendres and all. Then we have Doc Owens (Reiser), who appears in a position that we have learned to mistrust: the director of the evil corporation. And Reiser has a history with duplicitous characters in the genre, so when he says "Trust me," we all think, "Not on your life." But with both these characters, the series plays against expectations to a certain degree. And finally we have Bob (Astin), Joyce's boy-friend, who delivers *the worst* advice to Will on how to handle his problem, although he means well. He is such a charming and de-lightful character. Apparently he ad-libbed a number of his funni-est bits.

HW: The Brothers Duffer certainly seem to encourage that kind of thing. When you watch the related after-show, you get the sense of their abiding affection for their characters and cast, but also for their desire to deliver the best product possible. On the surface, it seems like a real family atmosphere. It bodes well for Season 3, for sure. What is evident to even the most casual ob-server of these two seasons is the sense of growth and expansion. The characters grow and change, and so does their world, with the aforementioned diversions provided by changes in locales and the expansion of the cast. The shoutouts to disparate influences continue to abound. There were definite Lovecraftian overtones, specifically to "The Colour out of Space," and to the existence of the so-called Old Ones. Overall, you get the impression that the Brothers are channeling everything they've ever seen, from *E.T.* to *The X-Files* to *The Goonies* to even older material, such as *In-vaders from Mars*. And let's not forget the overt and covert nods to the original *Ghostbusters,* whom the boys dress as for Hallow-een. The contentious debate between Mike and Lucas about who should portray Winston Zeddemore is hilarious, and teeming with subtext.

BV: Let's talk a little about the perturbations introduced this sea-son, the things that upset the ordinary lives of our ragtag group of heroes. For the boys, there's Maxine, a.k.a. Max or Mad Max, the skateboarding, Digger-playing girl from California who im-mediately draws their attention. Boys being boys, they act dumb around her and fawn over her, everyone except Mike, who re-sents the way she seems to be insinuating herself into their group. There's an element of jealousy, but mostly I think he sees her as a threat to Eleven's memory as the honorary female in their gang. In one scene, she critiques Lucas's account of what they're up against by calling his story "a little derivative," no doubt a poke at people who've made the same critique of the show.

For the older kids, there's Max's stepbrother Billy, who resembles a bad-boy rock-'n'-roll idol. There's a funny scene where he flirts with Mike's mother, but he's also a thorn in Steve's side and a torment to Max. On the supernatural, there's the creature who gives rise to the title of this piece, the "cute" little pollywog that Dustin adopts and calls Dart, short for D'Artagnan. Dustin thinks this creature (which rather conveniently first appears in the garbage cans outside his house) is his ticket to winning over Max, and he risks the bond with his friends when he hides Dart from them. Little does he realize what Dart will grow into—and that's not the worst thing they have to confront. There's this seasons BIG BAD, something straight out of Lovecraft.

HW: Yes, lots of complications, lots of emotional growth. There's a lot to do with parenting here, both good and bad. Eleven finds a new father in Hopper, moving away from her strange relationship with her "Papa." She in turn meets her aunt, her birth mother, and her sister in trauma, 008. Hopper tries to be a father to Eleven, risking a broken heart. Murray acts as a mentor/father figure to Nancy and Jonathan, guiding them in their battle against the authorities and urging them to pursue their smoldering feelings for each other. Bob, a good mate for Joyce, tries to give fatherly advice to Will and becomes the de facto man of the Bayer household. But for all the good, there's a lot of bad. Billy's dad is abusive toward his son, Dustin's mom doesn't have a clue, and Nancy and Mike's parents seem to be sleepwalking through their existence. And, of course, there's the most tragic couple in television, Barb's folks, the Hollands, who are dealing with the absence of their child by denying the obvious. The dinner scene between them and Steve and Nancy is just heartbreaking, as the kids, who long to tell the Hollands what they know, have to keep mum.

I also liked the move toward spectacle in this season. The scenes inside Hawkins Laboratory and the ever-expanding upside down (especially the tunnels) were gripping, and the looming presence of the BIG BAD, inching ever closer to our reality, is bound to induce nightmares in the more impressionable among us. All in all, I thought it was a fine stew, exploring many themes and nodding to myriad influences, all with good humor and an excellent sense of pacing and character development. I think a third season is definitely justified. Hopefully, the kids don't get spoiled, and the Duffers get even more money to lavish on production.

BV: You mentioned the after-show, which has become something of a requirement for "must see" series, and as far as they go, *Beyond Stranger Things* was pretty good. Seeing the way the young actors (and the adults) interact with one another is amusing. I chuckled at the way the Duffers busted Caleb McLaughlin (Lucas) for blowing his nose on camera. On a tangentially related note, check out the iOS and Android "8-bit" adventure game. It was surprisingly addictive. I haven't played computer strategy games since the era of Larn, Rogue, or King's Quest, but I enjoyed this one. It is closely tied to the TV series, and it gave me a better feel for the layout of Hawkins. Also, it didn't have any in-app purchase requirements: it is totally free, and it occupied me for about twenty hours in total.

And, yes, the series features young kids dealing with adult problems while the adults are mostly AWOL or clueless, but they are more present than in the first season. I got a kick out of Dustin's mother. It's clearly a close, loving relationship, and even when he deceives her it's for a good cause. I also liked the fact that she was apparently the lone Mondale/Ferraro supporter in Hawkins. Joyce and Hopper are the main adults who are aware of what's going on, and Joyce once again is forced to turn her home into some kind of art installation to get to the bottom of the mystery. I think I read somewhere that the Duffers promised that Joyce's house wouldn't be turned "upside down" (see what I did there?) next season.

I wonder where they'll go next season. They can't abandon the Upside Down, and there's a strong hint of that after that wonderfully nostalgic school dance, which has a nice bit of symmetry for Dustin and Nancy (who, as you may recall, slammed the door in Dustin's face when he tried to offer her a slice of pizza at the end of S01E01), as well as wonderful moments for the other kids. To what extent will the other Hawkins Lab subjects come into play, and is there an even BIGGER BAD lurking out there for the town—and the kids to contend with?

James Ulmer:
An Exponent of Quiet Horror

S. T. Joshi

JAMES ULMER. *The Fire Doll: Stories*. Huntsville, TX: Texas Review Press, 2017. 147 pp. $18.95 tpb. ISBN: 978-1-68003-127-0

James Ulmer appears to be one of the best-kept secrets in contemporary weird fiction. In spite of the fact that, prior to this current volume, he issued a collection of ghost stories, *The Secret Life* (Halcyon Press, 2012), Ulmer seems almost entirely unknown to devotees of supernatural fiction. There is no entry on him in isfdb.com, and I myself had never heard of him until he wrote to me directly, asking if I wished to read *The Fire Doll*. I am very glad I took up Mr. Ulmer's offer, for this book shows what a writer who—at least in a social sense—works outside our somewhat incestuous community can do with the age-old tropes and motifs of weird fiction.

Ulmer, currently a professor of English and chair of the Department of English and Foreign Languages at Southern Arkansas University, has in almost every one of the eleven stories in *The Fire Doll* chosen to work in the vein of what is somewhat misleadingly called "quiet horror." His smooth-flowing, lapidary prose, the honesty of his character portrayals, and his intuitive understanding that supernaturalism in a tale should be a symbol for the conveyance of reflections on the human condition all work to lend his stories a depth and meaning far beyond their surface events. And yet, apprehension and outright terror are not lacking, and Ulmer's expert management of narrative pacing brings nearly all his tales to a satisfyingly grim conclusion.

A fair number of Ulmer's tales focus on the complexities of interpersonal relationships, as a succession of men (a majority of his protagonists are male) find themselves caught in troubled or wrecked marriages, with the weird phenomena emerging precisely because of that circumstance. Prototypical is "Rendezvous Bay," where a man named Reed sees the ghost of his wife, Angela, while he is in the company of his new lover, Janet. Angela's very presence forces Reed to confess to Janet that he is not in love with her. The whole scenario is a compact metaphor for Reed's inability to free himself of his deep feelings for his departed wife. "The Luna Moth" tells how Jack Conroy sees, through a knothole in a fence, a beautiful woman disrobing in front of a man whose legs alone can be seen. Inevitably, the erotic image affects Jack's relations with his own girlfriend, to the extent that he has fantasies of beating and raping her. The conclusion of this tale is too clever to reveal here.

One of the lengthiest stories in *The Fire Doll* is "Safety Cove," about a man named Nick Wilmarth (no Lovecraftian allusion intended!) who moves to Tampa, Florida, to be near his sister, Anne, and also to the grave of his dead mother. When he is attacked by one of three cats he sees in the cemetery where his mother is buried, the adventure begins. It ultimately becomes clear that we are dealing with shape-shifting vampires—for what else can the alluring woman, Katrina, whom Nick meets in a bar be? And why was Anne later found dead, drained of blood? Although the latter stages of the tale become a kind of action-adventure narrative where Nick realizes he must put a body of water between himself and the female vampires who are pursuing him, the story is actually one of the fundamental loneliness of a man who has lost his last living relative and perhaps senses that much of the meaning in his life has similarly been drained.

A different kind of relationship is depicted in the other long story in the book, "The Fire Doll." Here, the police officers Richard Katrovas and Allison Reese have been lent to the FBI to investigate several murders of women in Texas and Louisiana. Allison is kidnapped by four or five men. Ten days later her captors are either killed or captured, and she is found naked and chained in the basement of a house. She commits suicide eight months later. Richard—who had made love to Allison at least once— must now face the trauma of carrying on both his personal and professional life in the wake of her death; and matters take a turn for the worse when the chief culprit in the case, the utterly ruthless Luther Mooney, escapes from prison. Richard pursues him and ultimately kills him—or does he? He himself tells his superiors the incredible tale that, while communicating with Luther by radio, he heard Allison's voice say, "Hello, Luther." At a press conference announcing Luther's demise, Richard thinks he sees Allison in the audience. When he approaches, she merely says, "Let me go"—in other words, Richard must forget about her so that she can find peace, and so that Richard himself can move on with his life. This richly textured tale, with every character vibrantly rendered, is compelling on a multitude of levels.

Other tales in the book are perhaps slighter, but not much less powerful. "Pine Straw" tells the story of how Clayton Talley moved to Loblolly, Arkansas, into the house of a woman who was found dead there years ago. He finds himself blanketed by pine needles; as Ulmer evocatively writes at one point, "He lived in a cave in a rain of pine needles." What else can this be but a symbol for his burying himself away from the turmoil of life? "Sad Annie" is a somewhat more orthodox ghost story in which a sad-faced girl leads a boy to a ravine where the bones of as many as twelve women have been dumped. The ghost of the girl appears later—smiling this time, for she has accomplished her purpose. In "Camden on the River," a married couple, Kate and Josh, visit a Confederate cemetery and see the ghost of Kate's father gesturing to them. The apparition appears to them several more times:

> . . . a figure detached itself from the shadow of the nearest pine and stood before us, as real as the crosshatch of branches or the mailbox tipped at the curb in apparent alarm. A dark suit, white shirt open at the neck, feet bare in the cold—the face livid, horrible, the eyes staring like glass. Shadows threw a pattern of diamonds over the pallid face and shirt front of the dead harlequin.

He had been a horrible, corrupt man in life, so it is perhaps no surprise that another ghost—that of Kate's sister—emerges later, pointing accusingly at him.

"Shadow in a Green Field" is a clever monster tale about a man found dead in the woods, his arm and leg ripped away. This does not seem to be the work of an animal, but no human being is strong enough to have done this kind of damage. The dead man was a photographer, and when the film from his camera is developed, a dark shape is seen in some of the photographs: "The picture showed half the features: one eye, completely black, and half a mouth full of long, thin teeth, the jaw unhinged like a piranha's, the lips gray." How is it possible that the photographer did not sense this creature approaching him with obviously sinister intent? Once again, the conclusion of this tale is too pungently effective to reveal here.

And one cannot pass over the book's final tale, "The Summer on Breckenridge Street," where David Lessing, feeling rootless and "dead inside," goes to Gettysburg, where he had gone to college, and senses the presence of the soldiers who had fought in that epochal battle a century and a half before. This is nothing more (or less) than an extended prose-poem, exquisitely evocative and poignant.

It should be evident that James Ulmer, beyond his other talents, has a deep and abiding love for the regions—mostly in the South—where he has lived and worked, ranging from Texas (he was formerly a Writer-in-Residence at Houston Baptist University) to Louisiana to Arkansas. The distinctive topography and culture of the South are evident on nearly every page of this book, contributing to the atmosphere of pensive weirdness that the author effortlessly creates. Eschewing the flamboyance of over-the-top bloodletting, James Ulmer has written a volume of weird tales whose meticulous craftsmanship and sureness of technique will prove far more enduring than the cruder, noisier contributions to our field.

Visions of the Abyss

Christopher Ropes

MATTHEW M. BARTLETT. *The Stay-Awake Men and Other Unstable Entities.* Introduction by Scott Nicolay. Interior art by Dave Felton. East Brunswick, NJ: Dunhams Manor Press, 2017. 93 pages. $23.00 hc. Limited to 150 copies.

On his Facebook page in 2016, Steve Rasnic Tem, a veteran horror, science fiction, and weird fiction writer, gave a definition of weird fiction that I think is pertinent to any discussion of Matthew M. Bartlett's work. Among the several paragraphs of Tem's description, two sentences leap out at me. The first states that weird fiction is "Dark fiction which eschews traditional tropes such as vampires, werewolves, etc. in favor of personal and idiosyncratic perceptions of the strange." The second: "Many of these tales seem to come from a broken place and are imbued with threads of sadness."

I can't think of a better way to describe Bartlett's newest book, *The Stay-Awake Men and Other Unstable Entities.* Bartlett's visions of the strange—and I do mean *visions*—are utterly personal and idiosyncratic and, despite dollops of dark and bleak humor, laced with thick strands of sorrow.

Following a rousing, insightful, and at times hilarious introduction by Scott Nicolay, Bartlett lures us into his unique visions of a deeply personal hell with "Carnomancer." LaFogg is a front-end manager of a grocery store with a secret he has been keeping even from himself. The titular "Carnomancer," or flesh diviner, is the former meat manager of the store LaFogg works in, a man LaFogg can't ever recall seeing before.

I see hints of Ligotti's "The Town Manager" in that aspect of the story, hints that create an atmosphere of sustained dread throughout the story. To be quite honest, I see a great deal of Ligotti influence in Bartlett's work, influence that is never derivative and is always filtered through the intensely personal lens that Tem mentioned weird fiction tends to utilize.

The dwelling of the Carnomancer himself is a perfect example of what I mean when I posit that Bartlett is showing us glimpses of his own hell. The raw physicality of meat and carnage provide the backdrop for LaFogg to discover the key to the secret he hid even from himself, and the revelation is shattering for LaFogg and the reader both. The core of sorrow in the tale is impossible to ignore when the final two pages of the tale are read and we realize just what is haunting LaFogg.

Next, "Spettrini" introduces us to Greyson, an aging magician who finds himself following a carefully laid breadcrumb trail that leads to his old teacher, Spettrini, in a shocking and truly horrifying manner. The last image the story leaves the reader with made me gasp, both for its imaginative force and for its powerful shredding of the illusionist's illusions about his place in the world.

"Following You Home" is a vivid and terrifying gut-punch of a story, almost microfiction, that relates to Tem's quotation about personal perceptions of the weird in both the creature that the narrator Merrill encounters and the nature of the specific hell that Merrill is left with at the end. It is an Abyss for him and him alone, and it could have come from no imagination but Bartlett's. I will confess that, after reading this story, I went for a walk, and I was jumping at every movement and shadow.

In "No Abiding Place on Earth," our main character, Daniel, embodies the essential sorrow of much weird fiction by a mysteriously damaged relationship with his grown daughter. Once again, there are creatures of unknown and unexplained origin, and they are among the most horrific creations that Bartlett has ever come up with. The ending is devastating.

"Kuklakar" reminds me of a Ligotti corporate horror story. The narrator tells us of his mysterious company, which introduces new management, a recurring theme in Ligotti, and the wildly inventive havoc they wreak. The loss of our human nature comes through as a fiercely frightening occurrence that lays waste to what we thought we were and replaces it with something heretofore beyond imagining. Is it for the better or for the worse? Bartlett makes it clear, both through what he says and what he doesn't say, that there is nothing more horrible than losing our humanity.

In the title tale, Don is in search of a recording of a mysterious radio broadcast that possibly gives clues to the disc jockey's disappearance. Don is obsessed with radio and is trying desperately to piece together the mystery. A brief lead-in to the main body of the story details an obsession with radio that may be Don's or may be the vanished disc jockey's. Few other clues to Don's interest are given, making it seem like a weird occurrence in itself. After a very private screening of a mysterious film somehow related to the disc jockey, Don discovers he is more intimately related to the disc jockey's Fate than he ever would have dared imagine.

Lastly, another borderline microfiction story, "The Beginning of the World," gives tantalizing hints of what being present for the birth of a new world would mean, and horrifies with the implications. The tale features another father and daughter pair (this time the daughter is a child), and what happens to them is the perfect closure to this small collection of magically terrifying tales.

Punctuating all the stories are heaping helpings of Bartlett's trademark humor, sometimes causing me to erupt in belly laughs despite the awful nature of the goings-on.

Mention must also be made of the spectacular Dave Felton artwork scattered throughout the book. Felton's work is a frequent feature of Dunhams Manor publications, and I cannot stress enough how much his work adds to the book as a whole. His drawing for "Following You Home" is a major part of why I was scared to death on my stroll.

I give this collection my highest recommendation. Using Tem's guidelines for what constitutes weird fiction, Bartlett is not only creating definitively "weird" literature, but he is among the leaders in the ongoing renaissance of worldwide weird fiction. I look forward to the hells he drags me through next.

Mantid: An Interview with Farah Rose Smith

Alex Houstoun

As has been covered in previous issues of this journal (see Ashley Dioses in *Dead Reckonings* No. 21—ED.) we, readers and purveyors of all things weird literary, have recently been blessed with a bountiful array of independent magazines, journals, zines, and other printed matter devoted to weird and unconventional literature.

To be added to that ever-growing group is *Mantid*, "a literary publication celebrating women writers and media creators from various background." *Mantid*'s mission appears to distinguish it from many of its contemporaries because of its explicitly stated mission to "serve as a platform for marginalized groups in the arts (women, LGBTQA, women of color, and people with disabilities/differently-abled)" and to "foster a diverse creative community and to bring unique, fiercely human voices to the forefront of modern weird storytelling."

Stuck by the intensity of the purpose behind *Mantid*, I reached out via email to Farah Rose Smith, the editor and publisher of *Mantid*, to discuss the publication and her process in compiling issues.

AH: Recognizing that this is an incredibly open-ended and somewhat frustrating way to start, I hope you might be able to explain and elaborate on *Mantid* and the philosophy behind it. You write on the *Mantid* Facebook page that the "ultimate goal" of *Mantid* is to "foster a diverse creative community and to bring unique, fiercely human voices to the forefront of modern weird storytelling" and that *Mantid* serves as a "platform for marginalized groups in the arts" with a particular attention to genre fiction. Why this particular area of art—in your words "weird fiction, horror, dark fantasy, magic realism, and dark science fiction"—and why now?

FRS: The ideological undercurrent to the project in the beginning was essentially that there are stories by unusual, under-appreciated, and under-promoted voices that deserve a platform, because they are not getting through via the normal storytelling or publishing avenues at the levels which they should. One problem that I can verify is that diverse writers do not submit enough, and sadly this stems from quite valid points and fears about exclusion. *Mantid* was never meant to be an isolated publication where diverse writers could go to, but rather, a platform for them to be heard among other known voices and then gain interest from other places (a goal which I can thankfully say has come true). I was especially attracted to the idea that the magazine would also appeal to diverse readers.

This all began with my personal frustrations being a genre/art filmmaker in a very commercial school in Boston, at the same time that I was beginning to take part in the Lovecraft community events in Providence, R.I. I became aware of vast canyons of perspective and interpretation that seemed to be more based on laziness and indifference than ideological ferocity (though I encountered that far more times than I would have liked to). This said to me that mere exposure to different kinds of art, culture, and storytelling could nudge people toward inclusion and innovation. While some people view this as an abandonment of past literary giants, or some kind of flag-waving political statement, I maintain my view on it as a natural, warm, respectable progression.

Now is the time because it has never *not* been the time. There may be greater courage to push boundaries toward inclusion and diversity because people are at points of frustration that cut so deeply that they must act, but there has never been a bad time for the undervalued to exist. As for the genre specifications, there are two answers, the less thoughtful of which being only that my personal fiction preferences leaned toward these genres, and my finding of sanctuary within them led me to believe that other oppressed groups had as well. The other reason is that the fantastical and weird have long been arenas of exploration for and of oppression, struggle, and fear. These themes are not special to one kind of person. However, the intricacies, roots, variations on fear and horror vary profoundly from person to person. Why not hear a different take on such things?

AH: Your phrasing that the genesis of *Mantid* began with your frustrations toward the laziness and indifference of some of the perspectives you were encountering coupled with this belief that "exposure to different kinds of art" can nudge people toward "inclusion and innovation" reads to me as if part of your intention with *Mantid* is to better those that originally vexed you. By "better" I mean to nudge them and make them more innovative. Is that a fair analysis? Did you have an audience in mind with *Mantid*, or was the focus more so providing a platform for those who you felt were not receiving their due?

FRS: "Better" is a word I try to avoid at all times, though the idea of educating an audience or society and creators themselves by opening them up to different perspectives is appealing (and necessary for cultural growth). But hoping for something is far different than harboring a direct intention. I planned the collections with hope for meaningful impact, hope being the operative word. I know all too well how this particular medium tends to flounder with limited reach and criticism. Having said that, some people can get all the exposure in the world and still hold only few things dear, or have particular tastes, and that is entirely valid! It was the malice in so many against different writers and topics that I found disheartening. The idea of dismissing that which has not been read, seen, heard, that seemed like a reality that could be at least discussed with direct engagement between disparate creators and readers. There is an ongoing conversation in weird fiction about the validity of new weird and the difficult topics of the authorial character of the long-dead. I am of the belief that you can observe and learn prior texts, enjoy them or not, have reasonable perspectives on creators, and build off of or away from them healthily, if that is the desire.

I did have hope that perhaps young horror readers, particularly younger (16+, or of reasonable maturity for the content) readers of all genders/diverse groups, would read the series, but getting the publication into arenas where they are accessible has been a challenge. This is why I would ask anyone who does enjoy the series and stories within request that their local library get a copy for their shelves. I wanted women to see that women are out there writing, and pushing for inclusion. Some will say the idea of a women-only publication is a problem in that regard, and that is a discussion that could go in circles forever depending on perspective, logic foundations, circumstances, etc. I have switched between perspectives as well over the years, but ultimately I found it to be a healthier approach to be out there actively creating communities for women to develop in and out of. The platform is meant to be a positive stepping stone for storytellers, period.

AH: In my reading, what you are describing here sounds like the process of "bettering" one's self: "I am of the belief that you can observe and learn prior texts, enjoy them or not, have reasonable perspectives on creators, and build off of or away from them healthily, if that is the desire." This process of "healthily" building reads as a means of betterment especially given that you are grounding it in a relation to observed "prior texts."

Would you be willing to elaborate on your reasons for wanting to avoid the word "better" in this context? Or is it not merely in this context?

FRS: My problem with the word is a universal one that bleeds into this arena of observation, I believe. Your assessment is correct, but there is a deeper problem with the idea of misinterpreting personal progression as it relates to the outside world, and it is these connotations that I often find demeaning and toxic to certain groups. So it is, perhaps, the emphasis on the word that I prefer to avoid. I may be better within myself for having read this or that, having learned something, but am I better than someone else, or hold more worth? No, and that is getting into dangerous territory. Those kind of vanity-laced motivations are of little value. Though this does touch upon the egoism of fandom culture within literature. An acquaintance can only read one book a year due to severe dyslexia, but their keen intellect, decency, and passion for literature is no less than a friend who reads over a hundred books a year. Is "better" a valuable term to use in observation there? There may be gaps in knowledge, but they may have been obtained elsewhere, by other means. Because there are people who don't or can't read everything under the sun for reasons that don't involve stinginess and indifference, I don't use the word better. It becomes a philosophical problem for me. But this gets me away from the context of the anthology, which was not designed to be representative of my personal philosophy. I try to remove myself from the conversation as much as possible because it is about the authors and their stories. This becomes a task due to aspersions people choose to cast for often unclear reasons that I inevitably must combat. People turn their nose up at women writing weird and horror fiction, and *that* is the problem. Perhaps that kind of opposition *cannot,* in fact, be altered with exposure. But is it worth a shot? Absolutely.

AH: My own use of "better" in this conversation was meant as personal—a personal betterment, not a comparison, or competition, between two people per the example of your friend. In that regard, I think we are speaking to a similar thing albeit with different language.

Returning to the original topic of our conversation, and apologies for the digression, the way you have described your role as the editor of *Mantid* appears to be paradoxical in a way I find interesting: you are the editor, you curate and create each issues, you are the editor, the publisher, and yet you write that it is not representative of you or your philosophy. I think this highlights a great challenge facing editors in general, that is, you are invisible in a sense but also responsible for what is ultimately presented to the readers. Can you talk about the process of putting together the first three issues?

FRS: No need for an apology! Language can be tricky and I try to be careful with it, or at least as sensible as possible.

I try to distance myself from being the type of editor who dictates and creates a very narrow window for material based on personal preferences. If it were a publication based on my tastes alone, it would have been archaic and decadent, and not served the purpose that it is meant to serve. That is not to say it is completely devoid of bias because nothing ever can be, but it was more important for me to speak to unconventional or ignored audiences. Having said that, that creates another difficulty because as a person of a particular identity, I don't necessarily know what different people want to read. I make the best calls that I can, and it is a learning process for me as well. Editing is tricky business, and I have always felt a distaste for certain strains of egoism that can seep into it. I rather think of myself as a facilitator of connections and material.

The first issue was put together as more of a traditional magazine with interviews, articles, photography, and fiction. It is ultimately a challenge to just "decide" to start a zine or anthology from the ground floor because one has to handle the pressure of both learning and doing at the same time. My initial team started this venture with what I can only refer to as subterranean influence in the literary world (none!). At that time I was still at Emerson College, and several of my classmates were a part of the overall production process of that issue. Also, at that time, we were still accepting submissions from all genders. It wasn't exactly what we had envisioned, but it was a pivotal stepping stone toward what the publication has become (and is still becoming). We did not receive the warmest welcome in the world, but it gained enough of an audience for a second issue to come about. That issue only contained fiction and photography/"art," and by that time my team had dropped away to full-time jobs and didn't have time to contribute to pulling it together. It was the first to have stories by women and nonbinary people only. The issue received greater attention, more criticism, and again, the possibility of a third seemed to be on the horizon. That one took much longer to create.

The third came about after a considerable amount of time had passed, including time that I spent getting to know other editors and how certain kinds of publications are put together. The decision was made to cut *Mantid* down to a traditional (albeit small) anthology, which seems to have been a popular and well-supported decision. The decision to make it a women-only anthology, however, has brought about (childish, tedious) controversy.

AH: You've touched on it a bit, but I am hoping you might be able to elaborate further on how your editing process has shifted as you've learned more and the constant battle of creating something for yourself or self-reflective and something for an unknown. I like this idea of you, or an editor in general, acting as a "facilitator of connections," but it also makes me wonder: is the reader supposed to be aware of the editor serving that role or is it supposed to be something subtle and unobserved?

FRS: I think the approach to *Mantid* was self-reflective in that it reflected values I share with many as a reader of fiction, and being a colleague of writers. It was best for me to tune myself in to the needs of contributors (to the best of my ability, which is often flawed) and tune myself out to a degree. I soon realized that my personal tastes were not going to cut it entirely for a progressive collection, and the goal was for the publication to continue. It required coordination and consideration, and an enormous amount of help from friends and colleagues who weighed in thoughtfully. Frankly, none of it would have happened without the enormous support I received from the weird fiction community (namely Sam Gafford, Gwendolyn Kiste, and Anya Martin, who have been fiercely supportive since the first issue). Certain types of editorial approaches had to be avoided, namely, it felt as though it would have been inappropriate to want to suggest content changes or significant narrative overhauls. Coming from a position of trusting storytellers, the idea that accumulating or aspiring toward some kind of despotic authority as an editor seemed counterintuitive (and distasteful).

While there is and should be a certain amount of teamwork between editor and writer, my idea is that if the editor is doing their job correctly, they should not be thought of at all by the reader. I am likely in the minority there. The title has grown into something of a vanity position in some cases, which may be necessary because it provides publicity for sales purposes if editors are well known, or take well to the social media/clout game in literature, but this has nothing to do with artistic or editorial integrity. I generally cringe when people ask me for interviews because, as a facilitator, I feel (in interviews unlike this one, where questions remain in safer, perhaps more casual territory that direct away from the purpose of the anthology) that I am doing a deep disservice to the contributing writers by putting myself in that position. In general, much like film editing, where a sloppy cut will take a viewer out of the experience, something that makes one aware of the editor's presence is usually a negative thing.

AH: Perhaps it is my own sensitive ego as an editor, but I would like to push back against the last point you make because, while a sloppy cut might take the audience out of the experience and make them aware of an editor not doing their job properly, an excellent composition can make one really appreciate the subtle workings of an editor.

The third issue of *Mantid* has recently been released and, without putting yourself in an uncomfortable, cringing position, can you speak a little about this particular composition?

FRS: That's fair. It wasn't an attempt to undermine editors. I think that appreciation is merited, it should be acknowledged. Certainly, everyone wants to know if and that they are doing good work, and doing justice to a story on behalf of the writers. But the stories come first, and problems arise when the appreciation becomes strangely overabundant for those who should be facilitating. I was more referring to the idea of the celebrity editor than suggesting that those subtleties are not to be commended. Though perhaps the inversion of the ego is its own negative manifestation that can be counterproductive. I can't anticipate many sharing my opinion. I find more comfort in remaining as a shadow figure because it allows this particular platform to provide for other writers as intended. I wouldn't expect this to be suitable for every publication, particularly in an atmosphere that relies on particular modes of promotion to get works sold. It seemed that the mission here called for an increased subtlety, which I initially thought would be more effective with a large production team, but that experiment struggled profoundly with the first issue.

Luckily, no discussion of the publication itself will make me cringe! The third volume is more uniform than the previous two, with some selections of science fiction and fantasy, but fewer deviations from weird and horror fiction. We were very excited to include stories from Gwendolyn Kiste, Brooke Warra, Carrie Laben, Nadia Bulkin, Victoria Dalpe, Kaia Hodo, Dodie Miller-Gould, and Kaia Hodo. Themes run the gamut from family and sisterhood to murder, isolation, persecution, and shame. The collection starts off on a redemptive note, but ends on an ominous one, which was (I believe) the most distinctive choice I made when pulling together this volume.

AH: Do you feel as if the third volume being "more uniform" is a result of how the stories organically interact with one another, or is it more reflective of *Mantid* coming into its own? Is it necessary that there be fewer deviations from the weird and horror genres or is that a happy coincidence in the case of this volume? How do you perceive this uniformity may reflect itself going forward?

FRS: If I'm being entirely honest, I find myself moderately contemplative about the fact that the collections never quite turn out as "weird" as I would like them to. But that is not an aspersion cast upon the collection or its authors. I am marvelously proud to be able to publish these works. There is an ongoing conversation about what it takes for a story to be considered "weird," and that perhaps can change the perspective on the stories as a whole. I believe that all three volumes lean more toward traditional horror storytelling, but this is reflective of what is submitted. The stories aren't monumentally cohesive, or at least are not interacting enough for them to feel like they are flowing into each other, but that is by design. That is to illuminate the difference in authorial voice.

I think deviations from genre norms or a central preferred genre is a healthy thing, but there is a great amount of care that must be taken in deciding what is too much of a deviation. I think this is something I am still coming to terms with as an editor. My hope is that the publication will continue to move toward a "New Weird" direction. That new approaches to old themes will be the foundation, with deviations here and there, rather than seeking a speculative thematic swath. But much of this comes from my decision not to assign specific themes, which in many cases, I feel can be somewhat detrimental to a platform intended to break down norms of focus, either narratively or thematically. I certainly have a much greater understanding of what *Mantid* is supposed to be, learning through interactions with authors, other editors, and artists. I am happy to say that a healthy amount of the original mission is still in place, and that it seems to be making an impact (however gently). It could not have happened without community interaction and participation, and for that, I am quite thankful.

AH: Recognizing that this is probably one of the more vexing questions that gets casually lobbed about these days, and in this field, but what does "new weird" mean to you? Or rather how do you, personally or as an editor, define or recognize "weird" as opposed to supernatural or "traditional storytelling"?

I feel I understand what you mean when you say that the collections aren't as "weird" as you "would like them" . . . there is this quality to weird fiction that, if you are versed to a degree in the subject, you just recognize it. What gets confusing for me is, if "weird" is something that can kind of be simply recognized, how does "new weird" build on that or differentiate? I am not trying to be obtuse or difficult necessarily, but this distinction between "weird" and "new weird" always makes me think—despite the fact that some folks have been very successful in articulating a difference—that, in saying, "new weird," there is an implication that "weird" fiction is old or dated.

FRS: While people trend toward anchoring their definitions of "the weird" in the works of Lovecraft and his contemporaries, I anchor my recognition of the genre from a platform of folks like Kubin, Hoffmann, Heym, Schulz, etc. with a Middle-European eye toward the intersection of the fantastic and the unusual. I think there is lot that is unexamined in the realm of Surrealism, Decadence, and Symbolism as it pertains to modern and historic weird fiction, or perhaps that it is an area of exploration that is unexamined in contrast with modern developments (which is something I am also attempting to build scholarly work within). Though it is not entirely absent. I recognize the weird through atmosphere, suggestion, absurdity, and the idea of ever-present questions pertaining to the content that linger on after reading . . . ones that are posed without emphasis or poor execution. I don't think that if you are asking "is this weird fiction?" about a story, that it is an automatic no, though it is the case (as I'm sure you know well!) that when something is just *weird,* you know it and it rings true immediately. I am of the opinion that Virgilio Piñera is the greatest writer of the weird ever to have lived, and those who are familiar with his works (or wish to become familiar) would get a sense of what my hope is for the eventual overall feel of the anthology series. My only real hard position in all this is that I generally reject the notion that all weird fiction must have something cosmic about it. I am not a fan of excessive categorization and subgenre definitions, but I do consider cosmic horror to be different from the weird, and perhaps what may be defined as monstrous and where that may manifest itself in weird fiction is another question that pops up from time to time.

I generally reject the idea of "New Weird" if it is a suggestion of extensive content/conceptual differences because I only see minor distinctions, and the change of name does little other than to differentiate the works from those of yesteryear, or perhaps for writers to distance themselves from writers/writings within the genre, historically. Works that are called New Weird trend toward subversion of aspects more readily found in fantastic literature, this is true. My perspective pushes me toward seeing that if New Weird must be accepted as a new genre, then there are two main aesthetic avenues that deal with that progression (hyperrealistic-"accessible" and absurdist-maximalism) and they may be considered distinct from weird fiction itself, but that still feels as though it is an uncomfortable distinction. Though that is perhaps another topic of discussion.

I find it to be counterproductive to the idea that weird fiction needs to be progressive and innovative if we begin to break it down endlessly into subgenres. To do so may be better for readers to navigate what they want to read, but it also runs the risk of taking away this very vital conversation itself, which is "what is weird fiction?" The question itself is valuable because from it flourishes an enormous amount of discussion. "New Weird" may be used to differentiate the historic pulp horror days and the modern literary horror era, both housed within the genre . . . but the idea of definition is overly cautious. And I hate the idea that some literature is better than others, because that which is complex or "literary" is not automatically better writing. The genre is revolves around the indefinable. That which is authentic is not fixed, perhaps. Having said that, that which some weird fiction as it manifested in the early twentieth century is certainly dated, particularly that which reflects the more atrocious viewpoints of society that had not yet been acknowledged as heinous. I don't dismiss controversial or dated works because if one is to learn and progress, one needs to know the history. But weird fiction is evolving and needs no change in title to continue. Key aspects can circulate in a narrative and provide a platform for new perspectives, but that alone does not merit an entire new genre.

As an editor, I struggle with selections because it seems that there is a lot of confusion about what merits the title of "weird," but I think this stems from timidity rather than ignorance. I do think that the collections thus far have leaned more toward supernatural and fantastic fiction, with a few weird insertions cropping up here and there. The goal is to move toward collections that are more easily considered weird. So how I approach it in theory/intent and practice/manifestation has yet to find quite the right balance, as of now.

AH: With regard to this goal, anything you would be willing to share about the next volume of *Mantid* or other projects you may currently be working on?

FRS: The goal is for the fourth volume to become more comprehensively weird, and I hope that contributors will not shy away from taking real chances. The publication is friendly to experimental approaches, and this is an aspect I hope to increase as we move forward. There are already a few authors who have agreed to contribute (as they were unable to last time), so the outlook is very positive for the volume. I hope that anyone who hesitated to submit to our open call will do so freely, as the intent is to promote new voices alongside the known ones.

I am also developing a "weird theatre" anthology and seeking a publisher for that project, but for now that is on slow boil and will likely not bloom until 2020.

AH: If one is interested in submitting, what is the best way to do so? Finally, closing this interview out . . . have you read anything good lately?

FRS: The main website has been discontinued, but any interested writers may keep watch on our Facebook page for updated guidelines and the next submission call. It will likely be posted in late Autumn. That is facebook.com/mantidmagazine.

I certainly have been reading quite a lot lately! Which is a relief, because I fell out of my usual reading cycle last year and it caused some anxiety! I just came out of a wave of reading decadent works and a few poetry collections (studying Georg Trakl for a hope-for scholarly piece) and the moderate emotional exhaustion that caused has led me back to my favorite work by Walter Moers, called *The City of Dreaming Books*. It's a charming, quite unique fantasy piece that I return to often in times of disarray. I recently finished reading *Member* by Michael Cisco in order to prepare myself for the release of *Unlanguage* (which is coming out soon from Eraserhead Press). I also recently read *Pretty Marys All in a Row* by Gwendolyn Kiste and was really enchanted by it.

Considering an Overlooked Jewel

DARRELL SCHWEITZER. *Awaiting Strange Gods: Weird and Lovecraftian Fiction.* Introduction by S. T. Joshi. Minneapolis, MN: Fedogan & Bremer, 2015. 276 pp. $39.95 hc. ISBN: 978-1-878252-75-3.

"And the dreamer wakes, from out of his dream, into his dream. In the dream of the man who was dreaming, the dreamt man awoke. *Pace* Borges. Like that. All is real, and nothing is real. Lao Tzu dreaming he is the butterfly and the butterfly dreaming he is Lao Tzu."
—"Envy, the Gardens of Ynath, and the Sin of Cain"

Darrell Schweitzer is certainly no stranger to the field. In addition to being a novelist, he has been a respected editor and non-fiction writer for some time, as well as a frequent contributor to various anthologies and magazines with short fiction and other pieces.

As a short fiction author, he has written dozens of stories in many settings and genres, but seems to have an affinity for fantasy tales and Lovecraftian narratives. A sensitive writer, Schweitzer—in addition to his vivid imagination—displays another key element in his work, which is his marvelous grasp of history. He frequently roots his pieces in exotic places and even exotic times, and this adds to the complexity and strangeness, in some cases, of the story itself. S. T. Joshi rightly points this out in his thoughtful introduction to this volume, as well as the careful craft that is obvious throughout this tremendous collection. Reading through this solidly built, handsomely designed hardcover from the venerable Fedogan & Bremer, one is struck by the scope of Schweitzer's stories in this regard; like any collection, some tales resonate with the reader more than others, but none of the stories are less than good, and a few ("Envy, the Gardens of Ynath, and the Sin of Cain," "The Eater of Hours," "The Last of the Black Wine,"

92   Dead Reckonings

"Ghost Dancing") are excellent. From ancient times to the present, Schweitzer is obviously at ease in a variety of scenarios and paints them vividly. He also displays a deft ability with characterization, and the quality of his prose is always disciplined.

Peppered throughout are some nice accompanying illustrations in black-and-white from the artist Tim Kirk, which lend a finished touch to the book, and is something that elevates the production beyond the typical digital fodder so much in fashion at present. There's just nothing like the heft and textures (and smell) of a real book in one's hands.

Overall, this outstanding tome makes a fine addition to anyone's library of the macabre, and demonstrates ably why Schweitzer has been lauded as one of modern weird fiction's better practitioners.

Drabbles of Dread

Dave Felton

BRANDY YASSA, ed. *100 Word Horrors: An Anthology of Horror Drabbles*. n.p.: Kevin J. Kennedy, 2018. 128 pp. $13.90 hc, $2.99 ebook. ISBN: 978-0-244-96512-9.

Take your favorite weird tale—perhaps one by Poe, Lovecraft, or King—and imagine what it would take to tell that story effectively in exactly 100 words. After a cut-throat amount of editing, how much of the characterization and mood would remain, what little of the familiar author's voice still exists to carry the tale and capture your imagination? Is it at all possible to scare readers with so little?

This is what *100 Word Horrors: An Anthology of Horror Drabbles,* published by Kevin J. Kennedy earlier this year, sets out to prove. Kennedy has published several holiday-themed horror anthologies of flash fiction, all edited by Brandy Yassa, but this appears to be their first collection of "drabbles," an even shorter, stricter form of microfiction. Coined after a word game mentioned in Monty Python's 1971 *Big Red Book,* the drabble grew out of British science fiction fandom during the 1980s and became more widely read and practiced as fan communities took to the Internet. Today there are podcasts, blogs, and Reddit threads dedicated to 100-word stories, and it is no longer practiced by fans only; drabbles have been written by Arthur C. Clarke, Isaac Asimov, Terry Pratchett, Neil Gaiman, and many others.

At first read, this anthology seems a curiosity. Read a second and third time, the drabble appears to be much more than a writing exercise; it is a discipline that requires strict control and a use of precise language, but with a greater chance of failure than normal fiction. The worst examples of drabble—and this anthology has its share—read like truncated stories, final scenes of a much larger piece, without even a context to imply what is missing. The writing itself in these failed drabbles is competent, perhaps even imaginative, but the authors' inability to grab the reader and throttle the mind, to point toward an unspoken and unsuspected evil, leaves no impact or impression on the reader, and the pieces are soon forgotten. In this case, the very length of the drabble is a weakness, for unlike the novel, which a reader can bond with over many evenings and remember for a lifetime, flash fiction occupies only the briefest of the reader's attention, which makes it imperative that the story create immediate drama to etch itself in memory.

The greatest successes in *100 Word Horrors* come to authors who set up an expectation in the reader's mind and thwart or subvert it at the last moment, much like a joke's punchline; the greater the surprise, the more memorable the drabble. Take, for instance, Matthew Brockmeyer's "Lightbulb":

> I'm trying to watch the Raiders game but my wife keeps nagging me to go down to the basement and change the lightbulb. It's first and ten on the twenty-two yard line with a minute left, and she's standing in front of the television in a dirty nightgown, hair a mess, wagging a finger at me, harping about how dark it is down there. "Yeah, yeah," I say, trying to peer around her, "I'll get to it." But there's no way I'm going down there. I haven't been down in the basement since I buried her nagging-ass there years ago.

Of course, it had to end that way, but you didn't know it until you got there yourself, for hadn't the wife been standing in front of the TV just a moment ago? Yes, a spectre of herself, you realize when reading it again, or an apparition conjured by the husband's guilty conscience. Or better yet, her animated corpse who refuses to recognize the "till death do us part" of their wedding vows. Brockmeyer's drabble can be all that, but it succeeds insofar as the ending satisfies, and the story seems as natural as anything you might read. There is no sense that "Lightbulb" was a larger piece of fiction whittled down to meet the requirements of the anthology; it feels as if it could never have been anything other than its 100 words.

There is a similar satisfaction to Lee Mountford's "The Betrayal":

> My heart is broken. Sarah, the love of my life, flaunts around before my eyes. She is on the phone, arranging a date for this very

evening. At *our* house. She giggles and flirts, caring not for me or for our relationship. I see now that my feelings for her are unrequited. All the times I kept her safe from the *wrong* kind of man was for nothing. Well, I will not stand for this betrayal. No more hiding in the attic, watching and waiting. Now is the time to reveal myself to her. And to cut out her heart.

The narrator, who the reader assumed is an unrequited love or an ex-husband, is revealed as the psycho in the attic only at the third-to-last sentence, and it leaves an impression upon readers that will bring them back for a second and third reading. In the instance of an unreliable narrator as encountered in "The Betrayal," the drabble's brevity is a virtue, for there is little time for readers to suspect and doubt.

There are other tales that are so well done that you'd never suspect the author was writing under limitations: Lisa Morton's "The Dead Thing," C. M. Saunders's "Coming Around," Jeff Strand's "Shock Collar," Georgia Lennon's "Cold Toes," Richard Chizmar's "The Man in the Black Sweater," and Michael A. Arnzen's "Baby Steps" are all great examples of good horror fiction and superb drabbles. William F. Nolan's expertise makes much use of short fiction by giving character to a serial killer through abrupt and concise language in "Another Tonight," a two-word title that suggests so much more: another drink, another pickup, another murder. Skilled authors can squeeze the most out of a drabble with titles—which don't count toward the 100-word restriction—with multiple meanings that play upon its story, like Adriaan Brae's "Consumed by Desire." Little things such as this can make a drabble shine above others.

In *100 Word Horrors,* seventy-one authors contributed 110 drabbles, and unfortunately, most of them lack the luster of the aforementioned successes, which only make those successful stories shine brighter. The most forgettable ones set up a kind of cause-and-effect that ends at the moment of death or some realization after death, without any subversion or rewarding punchline. Others dwell only in an author's voice, a sort of meditation on darkness that cannot be sustained long enough to impart any dread on the reader. But there are plenty of bad people doing bad things to other people, along with demons, vampires, kaiju, aliens, insects, and ghosts; and yes, there are two references to

King Kong, which earned him a place on the cover of a horror anthology, strangely enough. *100 Word Horrors: An Anthology of Horror Drabbles* is an uneven road with ups and downs and a few potholes, but it's a road that points upward for practitioners of the drabble form. Given a wider readership, the number of talented and diverse writers to try their hand at it will increase, and they will go on to craft more bite-sized horror stories for fans of flash fiction to relish.

The Theory and Practice of Satirical Criticism

S. T. Joshi

Over the years I have dabbled in what I have chosen to call "satirical criticism." I am by no means the inventor of this rarely practiced literary genre, but I like to believe that there are reasons—having nothing to do with the mere expression of bile and vitriol—why it may yield some benefits for readers, critics, and even the authors and works that are the objects of this opprobrium.

Satirical criticism involves the fusion of literary criticism—even in the humble guise of book reviewing—with satire. It is, of course, easy to poke fun at bad writing, but doing so in a way that justifies the term "satirical criticism" requires something other than insult or abuse; and the underlying principle—or, perhaps, the hoped-for objective—is to illuminate the deficiencies of a literary work in a particularly pungent manner so that its failings can be exposed to all concerned.

It would be difficult to specify the creator of satirical criticism, but in this country one of its pioneers was Edgar Allan Poe, whose various reviews are laced with vicious attacks on his literary enemies. Ambrose Bierce, perhaps the greatest satirist in American literature, was also a noted exemplar. Bierce did not write many formal book reviews, or literary criticism in general, but his journalism—which dwarfs his collected fiction and poetry many times over—is replete with towering condemnations of politicians, clergymen, and other worthies. Bierce is frequently regarded as an indiscriminate hater, misanthrope, pessimist, or what have you, but he did not consider himself such. When a contemporary writer, John Bonner, took him to task for what seemed to him mere billingsgate, Bierce replied keenly:

> John Bonner, does it really seem to you that contempt for the bad is incompatible with respect for the good?—that hatred of rogues and fools does not imply love of bright and honest folk? Can you really not understand that what is unworthy in life or

letters can be known only by comparison with what is known to be worthy? He who bitterly hates the wrong is he who intensely loves the right; indifference to the one is indifference to the other. Those who like everything love nothing; a heart of indiscriminate hospitality becomes a boozing ken of tramps and thieves. Where the sentimentalist's love leaves off the cynic's may begin. You have lived and written to little purpose if you have yet to learn why the good do not make the bad behave themselves.[1]

H. L. Mencken practiced satirical criticism with flair and panache, in the hundreds of review columns he wrote for the *Smart Set* (1908–23), *American Mercury* (1924–33), and elsewhere. From his earliest days as a reviewer, he evolved a fairly consistent and rigorous standard of what passed for good writing, and he was unremitting in his condemnation of what failed to measure up to that standard. Simultaneously, he recognized that a satirical flourish to his book reviews would not only make them entertaining to readers, but underscore the follies and absurdities of the work being reviewed. Consider a passage from his riotous review of a best-selling sentimental novel by one Marjorie Benton Cooke, *Bambi* (1914—*not* the basis of the celebrated 1942 film):

> A sweet, sweet story. A string of gum-drops. A sugar-teat beyond compare. Of such great probabilities, of such searching reports of human motive and act, the best-seller is all compact. . . . But do not laugh too much, dear friend, however hard your heart, however tough your hide. The mission of such things as *Bambi* is, after all, no mean one. Remember the fat woman— how it will make her forget that she is fat. Remember the tired business man—how it will lift him out of his wallow and fill him with a noble enthusiasm for virtue and its rewards. Remember the flapper—how it will thrill her to the very soles of her feet and people her dreams with visions of gallant knights and lighten that doom which makes her actual beau a baseball fan and corrupts him with a loathing for literature and gives him large, hairy hands and a *flair* for burlesque shows and freckles on his neck.[2]

As for me, generally speaking I unleash my satirical criticism

---

1. Ambrose Bierce, "Prattle" (*San Francisco Examiner*, 3 November 1895); in *A Sole Survivor: Bits of Autobiography*, ed. S. T. Joshi and David E. Schultz (Knoxville: University of Tennessee Press, 1998), 215–16.

in instances when I encounter authors or works that are, from an abstract literary perspective, so far beneath contempt that satire is the only recourse; at the same time, I continue to use the most rigorous tools of the literary critic in my analysis. As Juvenal of old said, *Difficile est saturam non scribere* ("It is difficult not to write satire" [*Satires* 1.30]). I began working in this mode in the reviews I wrote for *Necrofile* (1991–99), the predecessor to the present esteemed journal; that was when Ellen Datlow, in one of the introductions to *The Year's Best Fantasy and Horror,* referred to me as "the *nastiest* reviewer in the field" (her emphasis). I took that as a compliment.

Some tender-hearted individuals—even among my supporters—appear to believe that the *tone* of my "satirical criticism" is to be deprecated. They complain that I come off sounding "arch" or "pretentious" or "holier than thou." *People, the adoption of that tone was quite deliberate!* The essential purpose of satire is to provoke, to annoy, to irritate, to offend, even to outrage; and the fact that I appear to have done exactly that in blogs, articles, and reviews suggests that I have succeeded in my goal. But I do maintain that I have a more serious purpose in mind than merely dialing up a few zingers to hurl at the objects of my derision. Chiefly, I regard my satirical criticism as a kind of public service, whereby I fervently seek to save readers from wasting their hard-earned money on the rubbish that I eviscerate. What could be nobler than that? Okay, that comment itself was somewhat satirical, but not entirely so—and it underscores a truly serious point, especially as it applies to our humble field.

The plain fact of the matter is that criticism of weird fiction is still at a very primitive stage, and the number of critics who could be said to have the critical judgment, educational background, and (perhaps most importantly) the courage to direct an unflinching gaze toward the contributions in our field, both past and present, is woefully small. Some critics who may otherwise be capable of the job seem to feel that the very attempt to sort good writing from bad is somehow not a legitimate function of criticism, whereas I see it as its central mission. To a degree—but only to a degree—the decision as to what is "good" or "bad" is subjective; but one finds, both in this field and others, a general consensus among informed critics as to who the leading figures are, even if judgments on individual writers vary, and perhaps vary widely. As Lovecraft once said, critics of poetry may differ as to the relative merits of Pope and Shelley; but all sound critics of poetry will agree that Pope and Shelley are true poets whereas, say, Edgar A. Guest is not. Evaluative judgments are not meant to be prescriptive but suggestive: they are designed to provoke discussion as to what actually constitutes good writing, in the hope that other critics—as well as general readers—will be compelled to confront this fundamental issue head-on.

Ever since I entered this field in the late 1970s, I was struck by the amount of mutual back patting going on among fans and writers of all sorts. In part, this tendency was inspired by the perceived need to stay on good terms with leading authors, editors, and publishers in the hope of cultivating their favor and thereby advancing one's career; but in large part, I believed, it was simply a result of a lack of sound critical taste. This was, indeed, a chief motivating factor in my co-founding of *Necrofile*. I in particular, feeling no obligation to toady up to the bigwigs in the field, wrote blistering reviews of books I genuinely felt to be markedly inferior, especially if they were by popular writers whom others did not venture to criticize. I continue to write censorious reviews and articles today, even though they occasionally alienate certain writers to whom I would like to extend invitations to contribute to my anthologies. But I also write reviews (and articles) on authors and works I judge to be meritorious, including Ramsey Campbell, Thomas Ligotti, T. E. D. Klein, Caitlín R. Kiernan, Jonathan Thomas, Michael Aronovitz, Steve Rasnic Tem, Jason V Brock, and a host of others. And I never write satirical reviews of novice or insignificant writers, under the age-old principle that it is unwise to hit a fly with a sledgehammer—or, in modern parlance, to "punch down."

There has now developed, over the past several years, an even more distressing tendency for certain writers and their followers to band together in tightly knit cliques; these individuals are so terribly insecure that they cannot endure the slightest criticism, however well-intentioned or constructive. Or is it that they are actually convinced that they have already attained the pinnacle of literary achievement, and therefore that criticism of any sort is a kind of *lèse-majesté*? I have no idea. But whatever the cause, the development of these cliques is unfortunate on many levels. It results in extreme touchiness, resentment, groupthink, and all manner of other bad things that inhibit honest and straightforward criticism. I trust I may be pardoned for at times baiting these timorous folks. Given how quick they are to express blubbering outrage and self-righteous indignation, they easily fall into the trap I set for them.

It remains an unfortunate fact that there are few venues for the expression of honest criticism of weird fiction—fewer than there were several decades ago. We have reached a stage where, in the old adage, "everyone's a critic," if by that we mean that we are to take seriously the readers' comments found on Amazon.com, many of which (both the positive and the negative ones) are manufactured for the express purpose of puffing up or tearing down a given author or work, irrespective of the merits or demerits of that author or work. In other contexts, it is regarded as somehow "bad form" to speak harshly of a work, even if there is nothing at all personal in the review.

This will never do. Not all books are good; indeed, relatively few are. And everyone is *not* a critic: relatively few of us are properly trained in the principles of literary criticism or endowed with the all-important quality of *critical judgment* (i.e., the quality that allows us to distinguish the good from the bad, the original from the hackneyed, the scintillating from the mundane), such that we can pass an even approximately valid judgment on the work in question. The need to separate the wheat from the chaff is even more important now—when we are deluged with publications of a wildly varying nature from big presses, small presses, and authors who cannot achieve print except by self-publishing—than it was decades ago, when certain individuals called *editors* exercised a modicum of gatekeeping. So, if satirical criticism can drive some particularly boneheaded author to give up writing and become a more useful member of society, where is the harm in that?

Clive Barker—A Boy & His Rawhead: An Analysis of the Story and the Film

Randall D. Larson

"Rawhead it was called, because its head was huge, and the colour of the moon, and raw, like meat."

—*Rawhead Rex*

This is an apt description of Clive Barker's brand of modern horror fiction, which similarly rages large and drips with rawness.

Clive Barker is not a subtle author. The broodingly dark atmospheres of Lovecraft, Blackwood, Ramsey Campbell, and Charles L. Grant are not his to wield. Barker carries no chaste, shiny stiletto, he makes no neat incisions into the psyche of his readers. Barker's stories plunge savagely like a blood-encrusted spade, not slicing cleanly but gouging thickly into the fears of his readers, leaving them not with an icy chill but with shattered senses. Value and benefit are similar: by examining the things we fear, close up, vicariously and viscerally, the reader can perhaps better deal with them in real life, while enjoying the entertaining sense of shock and fright in the horror tale. But style and execution are universes apart. Barker is no gentle master of persuasion and diplomacy. He barges in, howling, chainsaw racing at full throttle, and he jabs it relentlessly at each and every one of his readers, just to make sure there is no misunderstanding.

There is no vagueness with Barker. He is brutally forthright. Utterly honest. Raw.

His 1984 short story "Rawhead Rex," published in the third volume of *The Books of Blood* and subsequently made into his first motion picture adaptation in 1986, is a good example of Barker's picturesque grotesquerie. It's a good, solid monster story, the kind of grand archetypal monster-versus-mankind-until-mankind-overcomes-monster tale that readers (and moviegoers) have enjoyed for years, but this one has Barker's unique stamp on it.

And yet, it's not all mayhem and entrails. Barker's tale, like most of his stories, is disturbingly graphic but not for its own sake. Barker doesn't stuff our faces into the cinder pit of corpses just to titillate us. There is purpose to his plunder and grist to his gore. It might be said that, in our modern era of high-tech horror, whether to be read or to be viewed, where no horror is left to the imagination, and all manner of acts can be seen in living (or dying) Technicolor on silver screen or silver disc, horror authors therefore must go to even greater excesses in order to create a successful story. This is not necessarily true, as the quiet terrors of Robert Bloch, Joseph Payne Brennan, Ramsey Campbell, Charles L. Grant, Thomas Ligotti, Les Daniels, and others have continually indicated. And Clive Barker isn't piling rotting corpse atop of rotting corpse or dangling, dripping limb atop dangling, dripping limb just to compete with the latest chapter of *Saw* or the continuing *Texas Chainsaw Massacre* saga.

Barker's artistic style is a heavy-handed one; it is no less well-crafted or artistic than less grisly minded authors. Barker doesn't beat around the bush; he tears right through it, leaving both limb and leaf in disarray behind him. His is a brutal style. A raw style.

(Note: Spoilers ahead.)

In "Rawhead Rex," Clive Barker displays this style to admirable effect in the format of an old-fashioned monster story. An ages-old pagan god with the death-metal name of Rawhead Rex is accidentally dug out of its rural England burial ground by a tired farmer. Instantly awakened, his rawal highness commences a rampage across the peaceful British countryside until a visiting Londoner discovers its origin and, with a pagan relic, puts him back in his place.

That's the easy synopsis. But in the midst of this fairly simple and fairly traditional storyline, Barker creates Real Characters, Honest Emotions, delineates a Convincing and Effective Plot, and generates some rousing-good Genuine Horror. Barker's narrative style is the kind of easy-going, journalistic style popularized by King and Koontz, Ellison and Etchison, McCammon and Matheson, and others of their craft. It's so unassuming that Barker's sudden assaultive descriptions catch us by surprise and their effect is doubly disturbing. Yet he creates images and feelings that are beautifully descriptive, powerfully related, and largely unforgettable.

Like some of the best monster stories, we are given frequent glimpses of the monster's point of view. This is not some lumbering, ravaging beast making mindless mayhem. We are given a front-row seat inside its own raw head, and its impure thoughts are quite discomfiting. When it first rises from its rock-walled tomb, grasping farmer Thomas Garrow's spade in its huge hand, Rawhead delights in his near-freedom: "Kingdoms for the taking. . . . After so many years, after the endless suffocation, there was light on his eyes again, and the taste of human terror on his tongue."

Barker continues to describe his story alternately from Rawhead's point of view and then from the perspective of the various townsfolk who come into contact with him. The doomed farmer, Garrow, looks up into Rawhead's pitiless maw, which he finds huge, like a harvest moon:

> God, that mouth. It was so wide, so cavernous it seemed to split the head in two as it opened. That was Thomas Garrow's last thought. That the moon was splitting in two, and falling out of the sky on top of him.

Barker immediately switches perspective, from that of the doomed farmer Garrow, to the viciously victorious Rawhead himself:

> Then the King inverted the body, as has always been his way with his dead enemies, and drove Thomas head first into the hole, winding him down into the very grave his forefathers had intended to bury Rawhead in forever.

In this way Barker emphasizes and sympathizes with the observations and feelings of his human characters, while developing the malignant character of Rawhead and hinting at his own insidious inner dialogue. Barker is a master at *showing* a story, not telling it. And he shows it very clearly through the perceptions of characters like Thomas Garrow, Declan Ewan, and Ron Milton. It is all very purposeful; building, bloodied plank by bloodied plank, a relentless tale of terror and a spectacular monster of horror.

Despite his violent ferocity, Rawhead is not completely without caution, as in the scene where he attacks the police car and its doomed occupants. Here the malignant creature is initially hesitant, confused and concerned about the unfamiliar roar of its engine and screech of its tires, but he overcomes his anxiety through the realization that his destiny in to regain his power over those who have usurped his demonic throne: "Rawhead swallowed his fear and prepared for the confrontation. The moon grew teeth." This last metaphor is typical of Barker's narrative: even in the grisliest of depictions, he propels his story and his descriptions along with sharp, artistically effective prose.

From the start, Barker emphasizes the pagan religion that lurks behind the scenes, behind Rawhead's position and purpose. Immediately describing him as the King, Barker imposes this sense of diabolical divinity upon the narrative and emphasizes that Rawhead is no mere shambling monster awakening from the charnel pits of prehistory. He is *King,* was and ever shall be. He was worshipped as a god by some ancient pagan people, and now he's back to claim his birthright. "Rex" is no simple surname. It's Rex in the Roman sense: Rawhead is sovereign absolute; and as such he bequeaths his terrible communion upon the countryfolk by consuming as many of them as possible.

Barker continues to provide religious references throughout the story, thereby underlining the pagan religion that gave birth to Rawhead and which figures both in his resurrection and his demise. The township in which the events occur is named Zeal. Barker compares the town's current state of terrors with the tranquility it enjoyed prior to Rawhead's coming by a reference to pagan astrology, describing a newspaper clipping reporting the recent deaths of "a Gemini, three Leos, a Sagittarian, and a minor star-system of others." Its Catholic church's staff are described using very formal religious titles and references.

When we first meet Declan Ewan, the Verger of St. Peter's Church, he is recalling Christmas, describing Santa Claus as "the first Lord he'd ever believed in," and in like manner, his belief in the Lord of his religion had likewise failed him. Like the Verger, St. Peter's Reverend Coot is also undergoing a crisis of faith. At one point he admits to Ewan that he once felt a presence like God (but *not* God), which gave him an unaccountable erection; in response, Declan tells him the story of Rawhead and admits to his own pagan faith. Coot isn't ready to embrace the monstrous deity yet, and faith in his own god is somewhat restored when he witnesses Ewan in a bizarre ritual with Rawhead, in which Ewan's ecstatic baptism in the urination of Rawhead is graphically described. The reader shares Coot's abhorrent distaste of the act as much as what it symbolizes to him: his colleague's terrible turning away from God and worshipping a fiendish demon.

There are also numerous references to sexual depravity and the correlation of sex with Rawhead's pagan religion. In addition to Ewan's baptism of piss when he converts to become an acolyte of Rawhead, Rawhead himself masturbates as he recalls past glories while defiling the town's church. Further references to ritual urination throughout the narrative reinforce this theme, up to and including the ultimate demise of Rawhead, which is accompanied by an involuntary, forceful emptying of the monster's mighty bladder.

After witnessing his verger's depraved disciplehood under Rawhead, Reverend Coot gags uncontrollably and is spotted by the monster-demon. Declan captures him and brings him unto Rawhead, like Abraham offering a sacrifice unto his God. Unlike the very graphic depictions of Rawhead's previous killings, that of Coot is kept off-screen, the reader given only a brief hint that lets his imagination fill in the details. Recalling Rawhead's inverted burial of the farmer Thomas Garrow, we are simply left with Coot being picked up by Rawhead and feeling as though the world had turned on its head. It is an effective moment of subtlety, a chilling counterpoint to the thick dollops of gore spread out elsewhere, and leaves the reader with an exquisite chill.

"Rawhead Rex" is a strikingly metaphysical story as it deals with religion head-on, a topic that has frequently woven its way through the author's work, often critically. The story's blood-soaked pagan religion depicts Rawhead as the godhead of ancient faith that had faded into historical obscurity, and Rawhead's attempts to regain his stature fails through elements of that same bygone religion. This is simply the story's setting and narrative context; it makes no statement against or in favor of religion or of a religion, other than portraying its deity as a bloodthirsty monster who is able to stimulate the alliances of weak-minded human beings. Both clerical characters in "Rawhead Rex" are struggling in their faith, Declan Ewan, influenced by the demon's power into forsaking his religion in favor of becoming Renfield to Rawhead's Count Dracula, while Reverend Coot, abhorred by witnessing Ewan's corruption, manages to restore his faith, albeit just in time for Rawhead to send him to meet his maker.

"I write religious fiction, though the phrase causes people to pale around the gills. Clearly fantasy and horror are often about the fundamental problems of existence. Horror itself is very often religious in its roots," Barker states in an interview with Sid Smith in "Horror's Roots: Writer Clive Barker on Good and Evil in the Modern World," published in the *Chicago Tribune* for May 23, 1993. "Where else can you credibly deal with the absolutes of good and evil or probe life beyond the grave? . . . Those are the same tools of the metaphysician . . . But what's maddening about the modern evangelist is that he assumes he's the only one who has God whispering in his ear. God also whispers in my ear." (For more examples of Barker's somewhat shifting views on the spiritual, see http://www.clivebarker.info/religion.html.)

After demonstrating the zealous violence of his monster, Barker introduces the tale's protagonist, Ron Milton, a design consultant newly displaced to an English hotel near Rawhead country while he awaits the completion of his new home. While Rawhead continues chewing up the scenery, along with a fair share of its residents, Ron, his wife, and two children enjoy the countryside and the local festivals until their own close encounter with the spike-toothed Rawhead. Milton gets a hint of the murders in Zeal when Detective Sergeant Gissing tells him about the savage murders discovered at the Nicholson Farm.

Milton's wife Maggie insists that they return to London to avoid the menace of the unknown killer. En route, young daughter Debbie feels the call of nature. Milton pulls over and Maggie directs her behind a bush to relieve herself (another urination reference, although relieved of its ritualistic connotation). When Debbie cries out, Milton along with Maggie both rush to her aid; but she has only been frightened by a dead mole on the ground. However, back at the car, son Ian sits alone in the back seat, reading a comic . . .

> Suddenly, it went dark. He looked up from the page, his heart loud. At his shoulder, six inches away from him, something stooped to peer into the car, its face like Hell. He couldn't scream, his tongue refused to move. All he could do was flood the seat and kick uselessly as the long, scarred arms reached through the window towards him.

Ian's perspective here, colored by phrases like "[the mouth] smelt like the dustbins at the back of the school canteen, times a million," provides an effective and sympathetic contrast to the viewpoints of the others; and the varied perspectives of Barker's characters, fitting their age and personality, makes the story all the more real.

Barker potently captures a father's horror as, returning to the car, Milton confronts Rawhead in the act of consuming his son:

> Ron had never screamed in his life. The scream had always belonged to the other sex, until that instant. Then, watching the monster stand up and close its jaws around his son's head, there was no sound appropriate but a scream.

And later, after getting poor results from an impotent police service, Milton decides to talk to Reverend Coot about the demon that destroyed his son, describing the boy's destruction in heartbreaking detail. With the same kind of furious, raw narrative that Barker employs to convey his scenes of violent carnage, Barker effectively and profoundly illustrates the shock, horror, and anger of a grieving father.

Later, after Rawhead's assault on Reverend Coot, Milton finds him dying in the ruined vestry; Coot tells him that the thing is afraid of something in the altar. Milton confronts the mad acolyte Declan Ewan in the sanctuary, and after a fight the disciple is subdued. Beneath the altar, Milton finds a stone— some pagan relic protected from the ages, apparently hidden there by the same people who had buried Rawhead alive centuries earlier.

At this point Barker moves from straight supernatural horror into a kind of high fantasy as Ron confronts Rawhead, pitting the uncertain power of the "magic stone" against the monster's gruesome might. Like a crucifix against a vampire, a silver bullet against a werewolf, a villager's torch against Frankenstein's monster, the stone is a symbol of all that Rawhead fears, and as such it is a forceful weapon against him, one that gives the narrative a striking at Rawhead's pagan religion: "To him the stone was the thing he feared most: the bleeding woman, her gaping hole eating seed and spitting children. It was life, that hole, that woman, it was endless fecundity. It terrified him."

Rawhead Rex, perpetrator and purveyor of death, malevolent monarch and terrible tsar, is frightened into impotency by the image of life—the fertile woman. Excreting in panic, Rawhead backs away from the stone. With imagery from dozens of Frankenstein films in mind, a pressing crowd of villagers arrives and takes advantage of the monster's weakness to overcome him with fists and hand-wielded weapons. As Ron delivers the death blow, Barker gives us our final glimpse into Rawhead's mind as it dissipates unto death:

> There would be no resurrection this time, no waiting in the earth for an age until their descendants forgot him . . . He . . . looked up [at] the little father. . . . [but] now Rawhead's look had lost its power to transfix. His face was empty and sterile as the moon, defeated long before Ron slammed the stone down between his eyes. The skull was soft: it buckled inwards and a slop of brain splattered the road.

Barker leaves us with one final image, reinforcing the basic themes that ran throughout the preceding tale: "It went unnoticed, but in death Rawhead's bladder was emptying . . . After a few feet it found the gutter and ran along it awhile to a crack in the tarmac; there it drained off into the welcoming earth."

And so the greatest monsters always fall, not with a bang, but with a whiz. Barker's "Rawhead Rex" remains a compelling and effective monster tale, equal to the best of them. His themes in this terror tale—religion, ritual-and-sex, fertility and destruction, parental heroism/parental impotence, life and death—are effectively captured in a bloody inventive monster tale. Rawhead is a believable monster (partly because he is delineated in full dimension, given a history and personality of his own), and the story is a notable reworking of the classic archetype horror-monster story.

Scripted by Barker himself, the motion picture adaptation is entertaining but largely without style and a budget far too insufficient to give the story its due; in fact, Barker subsequently disowned it. In the film version of *Rawhead,* the monster is frightening in appearance, with a striking makeup that gives him an enormous head with thick hair brushed back and a gigantic mouth full of sharp teeth; it is an awesome prosthetic appliance but, with a few notable and very good exceptions, it remains a frozen still-life in the active visual medium. The monster's noticeable lack of facial movement even when roaring loudly belies any sense of reality, and Barker thought it was laughable.

Barker's script is faithful to his story, with a few changes, some of which were reportedly imposed upon the screenplay by others. The locale is switched to Ireland, and the protagonist is modified to a visiting American writer named Howard Hollenbeck (David Dukes), committing research on the "persistence of sacred sites" (as in Ireland's historic churches and burial grounds). He is accompanied by his wife Elaine (Kelly Piper) and two children, and his interest in inspecting Reverend Coot's church leads to his confrontations with Rawhead.

The film is directed by George Pavlou—this is one of four directorial credits, including *Transmutations* (1985), with story and screenplay written by Barker, but largely changed by the director and a second screenwriter into something that barely resembled what Barker wrote.

Rawhead Rex would be a second disappointment. The production's low budget and insufficient time frame caused much of Barker's purposeful scripting to be dispensed with in favor of uninspired rewriting and reworking. An enormous actor named Heinrich von Schellendorf wore the Rawhead suit for long and medium shots; its bulk prevented much movement. An animatronic puppet was used for close-ups. Makeup effects technician Peter Litten was in charge of the facial movements, but his request for a twelve-week shoot to refine the monster suit's animatronics were denied, since principal photography was only scheduled for seven weeks.

"I went to Litten's workshop to see the Rawhead figure, and I thought it looked like a gorilla," Barker states on *The Clive Barker Podcast* on February 2, 2015 [www.clivebarkercast.com/2015 /02/02/weekly-5-the-5-weirdest-clive-barker-adaptations/]. "On film I thought it looked like a wooden piece of effects work and when it lumbered along like an Arnold Schwarzenegger clone it killed the movie stone dead."

Pavlou's direction has its moments and is technically capable but fairly pedestrian. It is lacking an engaging visual style or nuance; camera set-ups and movement are uninspired, and the film's lighting bathes most sunlit or indoor scenes in a flat wash.

Nighttime scenes in the graveyard with Declan being baptized by Rawhead's urine fare much better. (The film's recent 4K restoration on Blu-ray gives its sound and visual image a spectacular crispness in comparison to its murky VHS and DVD presentations.)

Orchestral and electronic music by Colin Towns (a keyboardist formerly with the Ian Gillian band, whose debut score for *The Haunting of Julia* [1977], a.k.a. *Full Circle,* gave him much deserved recognition in film music circles), good performances by Dukes and particularly Ronan Wilmot as a suitably insane, corrupted Declan O'Brian, along with a capable supporting cast, makes *Rawhead Rex* the movie an entertaining and frightening affair. The storyline follows the same pattern as the narrative tale up until the ending, opening with the farmer digging up a phallic-shaped stone monument, intercut with shots of Hollenbeck driving his rented van toward the old church. When Hollenbeck arrives at the church, the choir is heard singing the hymn "All Creatures of Our God and King"—an ironic (and probably purposeful) selection in view of Rawhead's status as both monster-creature and demon-king.

Pavlou does accomplish an effective moment when Declan O'Brien leads his congregation in the aforementioned hymn: there is a stained-glass window depicting Rawhead being defeated and buried in the cemetery; sunlight filters in through multicolored window; and a fog effect shows the two rays of crimson sunlight shining through its eyes and into the church, with the camera's movement making the rays rather tellingly pass right across the figure of the verger. (O'Brien's Damascus-Road moment with Rawhead will similarly be fogged in a red mist, making the earlier scene an intriguing precursor to his fate.)

In his script, Barker dispenses with the internal perspectives of his monster and instead gets the story going at a fast pace, detailing his tale visually. Instead of the slow and moody point-of-view musings of Rawhead as he waits for Thomas Garrow to unearth him, in the movie we simply have Rawhead leaping majestically out of his tomb, wet earth sloughing off of him in brown cascades.

Rawhead's attack on the pregnant farmer's wife (a new scene not in the story) is quite good. With a furious pacing that captures her terror and panic, her helplessness is contrasted with

Rawhead's unstoppable onslaught. The monster's makeup is effective here: his bulbous, slant-domed forehead and cavern-wide mouth glinting with razor teeth (we'll forgive the sparkling eyes for the moment) are truly frightening; and the movements of actor von Schellendorf inside the monster suit are suitably relentless. Barker adds an interesting precursor to the story's ending: the woman here happens to be pregnant, a fact that Rawhead notices as he is about to rend her, and which stops him abruptly. He sheathes his claws, like a cat, and departs the house without a sound. The monster's fear of the female womb has rendered him impotent, a point that will be made plainer at the film's end.

A pair of new characters are introduced, young lovers in a trailer park surrounded by a forest of tall trees. Rawhead makes his dinner of a few of them, including the girl's boyfriend. An unrealistic but nice shock-moment is achieved when the girl and her boyfriend run, hand-in-hand, from the monster in the woods; the girl reaches the relative safety of her neighbors, not realizing until she holds it up that her boyfriend is no longer attached to the hand she clenches so tightly in her grip.

Hollenbeck becomes involved on the ongoing murders when he catches a glimpse of Rawhead on a hillside trail, staring at him after his visitation on the coach park. Unnerved by his creature's monstrous appearance and furious gaze, Hollenbeck goes to the police with its description. They naturally scoff, until survivors' reports from the trailer park match his account. Accepting the possibility of some unknown beast, the police investigate. Detective Gissing (Niall O'Brien), who leads the investigation, meets Rawhead face to face—although, whereas in the book Gissing and his driver are killed, Rawhead here mesmerizes Gissing and makes of him a slave. In the later confrontation between the police and Rawhead, Gissing shows up and torches a few squad cars and policemen before being engulfed himself.

The death of Hollenbeck's son (here named Robbie, well played by Hugh O'Conor) occurs just as in the short story, while sis is off making business in the bushes, and Dukes effectively captures the kind of tortured feelings Barker described in the story. It's a strong scene, the monster's most savage killing, and links Rawhead and Hollenbeck in a pact that will inevitably lead to Hollenbeck's final triumph. But the visualization of Rawhead in this sequence is, again, unexciting: the monster's toothy mouth a frozen tableau of teeth sprouting out in all angles like a bouquet of sharp bones beneath glowing nightlight eyes. Once more, aside from its frightening monster design, he appears to have all the ferocious power of a store mannikin in action.

Dissatisfied with police inactivity, Hollenbeck visits Reverend Coot (Niall Toibin) and inspects the church, where he has an unpleasant encounter with the verger, here called Declan O'Brien, who from the start appears less righteous than one would expect a catholic verger to be. Already he is spouting Rawhead-piety, as he tells Hollenbeck: "They burned him alive, the devil's thought they'd won. But the dark Lords come back. They always do!" Ronan Wilmot maintains an effective Dwight Fry/Renfield frenzy, just short of being overplayed, to his performance as Declan.

Soon, as in the short story, Declan will become Rawhead's acolyte, confirmed by bladdered baptism, and his witnessing this dooms Coot to destruction. In a final confrontation with Coot, Declan screams, full of ecstatic, almost pseudo-coital zeal, "He was here before Christ, before civilization! He was King here! Rawhead, that's what they called him! He IS God!!" When attacked by Rawhead, Coot holds up a small wooden cross in hopes of dissuading the demonic beast, but Rawhead crushes it into smithereens. Barker here not only demonstrates Rawhead's non-Christian origins but subtly suggests that his monster has nothing to do with traditional religious iconography.

Hollenbeck notices the stained-glass window in the vestry (the sunlit one from the earlier scene), which depicts an image of Rawhead being crushed by a robed figure holding a shining sword. Hollenbeck reads the Latin text beneath the window: "Death walks fearing what it cannot be"—a cryptic reference associated with the story's theme that Rawhead, purveyor of death, fears the seed of the woman.

The ending of the film is significantly altered from that of the story. Rather than being reduced to impotency with the kryptonite-like subduing effect of the relic stone, in the film Hollenbeck discovers that the stained-glass window depicts Rawhead's previous demise at the hands of an ancient warrior. But the window, having been repaired after previous damage, is missing the piece that shows the weapon. Discovering the piece on another restored window, he ascertains that the weapon is an ancient stone, here matching back up with the story.

Led to the altar by the dying Reverend Coot, Hollenbeck finds the "magic" stone bathed in a fog of glowing light. Wielding the lumpy rock, Hollenbeck confronts Rawhead in the church's graveyard, but his efforts have no effect. The "magic" stone seems as impotent as any of the monster's savaged victims. But when Hollenbeck's wife Maggie shows up in search for him, she takes the stone and instantly vanquishes the monster in lightning strikes of white, ethereal light and the ghostly image of a robed, hooded woman. Hollenbeck realizes another piece missing from the stained-glass window held the secret: "It had to be a woman!" The film concludes by supporting the story's theme of Rawhead's powerlessness against the symbol of life and motherhood.

The ground caves in and buries Rawhead beneath heaps of cold earth and stone.

The movie can't resist one final, typical cinematic shock: an epilogue portrays the graveyard, quiet and still. Suddenly Rawhead's huge, howling, fanged head lunges into view. Fade out to the End Credits, under Colin Towns' brisk finale music. The obligatory epilogue is unnecessary and contradicts the preceding story, and was evidently inserted in keeping with the then-current vogue in horror films for a final jump scare in which the monster, screaming, suddenly appears again at the very end. It's an unfortunate acquiescence to the exploitative that cheapens the narrative, falsifies the actual ending, and is out of keeping with the style of what has gone before.

Aside from that, and as both story and movie, *Rawhead Rex* is an entertaining monster tale if one can forgive its imperfections. As an example of Clive Barker's way of horror-telling, the story is a notable icon, demonstrating his style and characteristics within a fairly traditional type of monster story. As a film, while Barker was not as deeply entrenched as he was in the succeeding *Hellraiser* (an ensuing horror masterpiece that he also directed), the adaptation is faithful and similarly demonstrates his storytelling themes amid the standard kind of cinematic monster movie. The movie drips with Barker's style and ideas. Withholding nothing, they slam the reader and/or viewer smack in the face with a 50-pound slab of red meat. Stephen King, in his frequently emblazoned cover blurb, states: "I have seen the future of horror. Its name is Clive Barker." To a certain kind of horror—Barker's kind—he may well be right, and a new wave of authors influenced very much by the Barker style has emerged in the subsequent three decades.

When it comes to full-blown, explosive fear and fright, Barker's lunge-and-rip-out-your-jugular horror stories very much characterize the contemporary, ultra-graphic style of modern horror. They hold no punches, contain no furtive shadings, no subtle whispers of apprehension. They seize with vibrant horrors, rage with grotesquery, open up the sarcophagus and let what's inside slop into view in full, brightly lit color. Barker reveals everything to all the senses. Thrusting his hands into its squishy middle, he spreads the ghoulish things apart so we can see more clearly.

Barker's horrors are brutal, alive . . .

Raw.

Author's Note: In 1994 HarperCollins UK printed a 96-page graphic novel interpretation of "Rawhead Rex," with artwork by Les Edwards. It went out of print in 1996 and copies on secondary markets are pretty expensive. It's a provocative adaptation of the story. It would also make an outstanding storyboard for a cinematic retelling of Barker's original story.

A Letter Concerning Things Past

Acep Hale

Der Orchideengarten. Edited by Alf Von Czibulka. Translation by Helen Grant. Restoration by Jonas Ploger. Düsseldorf: Zagava Books, 2017. 28 pp. €18. ISBN: 978-3-945795-18-7.

My dear unknown friend,

Der Orchideengarten was a periodical that published its first issue in January of 1919, four years prior to the start of *Weird Tales,* which began publication in March 1923. *Der Orchideengarten* ran for fifty-one issues before ceasing publication in November 1921 and is considered to be the world's first fantasy magazine. In 2007 Zagava discovered two bound volumes of *Der Orchideengarten* and set about the arduous process of restoring the vibrant colors used in printing the magazine's covers and removing the effects of nearly one hundred years of aging.

These steps accomplished, Zagava replicated *Der Orchideengarten*'s original paper size (the Zagava edition's sheets are 30.4 cm by 22.0 cm, slightly larger than A4 format) and, likewise, the paper weight is as close as possible to the paper weight used in the 1919 deluxe edition of *Der Orchideengarten.* When I reached out to Jonas of Zagava, he provided these details as to the paper used in the printing of the Zagava reproductions: "There are actually two sorts of paper used in our edition: the facsimile part is printed on a slightly tinted working printer paper with an open surface which comes pretty close to the kind of paper used nearly 100 years ago. The translation sheets were printed on untinted, 'colder' paper in a modern font (Akzident Grotesk) to clearly emphasize the difference between old and new."

Which brings us to another delightful point regarding Zagava's reprinting of this issue of *Der Orchideengarten.* The contents of the magazine, including the issue's inner cover advertisement, have been charmingly translated from German to English by Helen Grant, so that those who do not read German may still read the translated text in context as the magazine's editors originally intended. Zagava bound vertical half-pages with the English text alongside their German full-page counterparts, and so the translated text lies alongside the artwork it was originally intended to accompany. This attention to detail shows the love and consideration Zagava has taken when approaching its task.

Der Orchideengarten opens with "Dream" by Rudolf Schneider, illustrated by Willhelm Heise. In this piece, the dreamer finds himself in a landscape quite desolate and bleak, goaded on by his well-dressed and respectable guide to shoot a bow and arrow into a crowd of innocents lest he himself become a laughingstock. "Dream" is a compact piece that is easy to gloss over upon first reading . . . yet I found my mind returning to it again and again, considering the themes at play and the time in which it was written, and I was soon researching Rudolf Schneider and his life. "Dream" proves an effective fragment that burrowed into my psyche and has now taken permanent lodging therein.

"18.XII 18." by Paul Frank, illustrated by Paul Neu, deals with a man's attempts at returning a dropped diary page, only to find himself fulfilling the appointments detailed upon this stranger's page. This period's fascination with the theories of Bergson, Freud, and Nietzsche haunt all the stories in *Der Orchideengarten*. Bergson, with his view that thinking distorts experience and his stress upon intuition being the one true guide to apprehending the entirety of the world around us, was at one time a widely read and highly influential philosopher. Freud at the same time was upending humanity's understanding of itself with a concept he himself was still struggling to shape, the theory of the unconscious. Contrary to perceived wisdom at the time of Freud's writing, human decisions did not arise from calm, reasoned calculations; instead, human beings reacted instinctively, primarily from a hidden reservoir of repressed memories of which they were unaware and to whose effects they were blind. Freud based a large part of his efforts to tap into this unconscious on dreams, which until then had been largely ignored, dismissed as the brain replaying scenes from the preceding day. Now dreams became rich fodder for exploration, as did the unconscious itself, as seen in Schneider's "Dream" and Paul Frank's "18.XII 18.," where the protagonist's personality takes on the tasks detailed in a stranger's diary page. Nietzsche removed society's final sense of security, arguing that the time of humanity's reliance upon the church as its basis for moral guidance had come to an end. He wrote that human beings must instead look within themselves and shoulder the responsibility for the creation of their own moral codes. Outside of *Der Orchideengarten* one can see the influence of these three thinkers within German Expressionism, the most widely recognized examples being *The Cabinet of Dr. Caligari* (1920) and *Nosferatu* (1922).

The revolutionary changes taking place in all spheres of society during this period of time are astounding to consider. Nearly every form of technological breakthrough we now enjoy has its roots in the end of the nineteenth century and up to the 1920s, from the telegraph to the typewriter; and the social upheavals that accompany such breakthroughs were felt by the souls involved in the creation of *Der Orchideengarten*. This was a fantasy magazine published in January 1919 by people living in Germany when World War I ended on November 11, 1918. The gift of being able to read others' responses to these upheavals is not one that should be taken lightly. I may be engaging in hindsight, yet the themes within Schneider's "Dreams" are chilling when one looks back with an eye to history. Motifs of mesmerism, unconscious forces, and the overwhelming social pressure exerted by crowds occur repeatedly within the small selection of tales selected for this inaugural issue of *Der Orchideengarten*.

"Master Jericho" by Karl Hans Strobl is the most straightforward tale within the magazine, detailing the exploits of a church organist and the mesmeric sway he holds over all who hear him. Because of Strobl's embrace of German nationalism, he has not been widely translated into English. To my knowledge, "Master Jericho" only exists within Joe Bandel's translation of Strobl's short story collection *Lemuria*. "Master Jericho" is an exemplary piece of Strobl's work by which to become acquainted with the man's highly evocative, lustful style.

This story also exemplifies the confluence of influences and motifs within *Der Orchideengarten*. The town's kindly organist is replaced by a mysterious, demonic outsider possessed of a dumpy body with long, spindly legs, a wild mop of green-gray hair, and horrible, talon-like hands encrusted with dirt. Despite Master Jericho's unfortunate appearance, he plays the church organ with such mastery that the town soon becomes a musical Mecca, and even those who try to stand "sufficient unto themselves," with "the anger of Prometheus," are overcome by feelings of religious awe. The story soon turns to traces of vampirism as select townspeople's *élan vital* slips away, and even death is no escape as a series of grave desecrations rock the community. The social pressure exerted by crowds is expressed twice within this brief tale. I have seen it written that Strobl sits at the crossroads between E. T. A. Hoffmann and Hanns Heinz Ewers. I find this to be an apt and fitting description.

Max Rohrer contributes the poetic ode "Bats," followed by a reprint of Victor Hugo's "The Way to the Scaffold," still quite a chilling account of a convicted man's last hours before climbing the steps to meet Mme. Guillotine. I wrote in my commonplace book while reading this piece, "Read Hugo once again." If *Der Orchideengarten* does nothing but convince people to return to Victor Hugo, I'll consider it a successful enterprise. A. M. Frey's poem "Nocturnal Visitor" follows, performing the remarkable achievement of conjuring William Hope Hodgson in a mere eight stanzas.

Following this is Dr. Max Kemmerich's "The Greenhouse: The Weird and Wonderful," a column of items such as "Mysterious music" and "Makeup and facial powders." "The Greenhouse" reads very much like columns such as "Strange Facts from Around the World," and I feel confident readers would be familiar with it in contemporary settings. That said, I was deliciously charmed by it and sincerely believe more than a few writers will discover rich sources for future stories within this collection of oddities.

The volume closes with two book reviews, both concerning works by individuals who contributed to *Der Orchideengarten*. It is reassuring to see that acts of hagiography masquerading as reviews are not a modern phenomenon, but rather a facet of weird fiction that has existed since the very beginning.

I would be remiss if I did not mention the stunning artwork in *Der Orchideengarten*. Starting with the striking three-color (black, red, and yellow) cover image of a blood-engorged orchid bursting forth from a greenhouse beset with impish figures, the magazine bears witness not only to the original artist's skill but also to the care and expense that Zagava has taken with this project. The interior etchings and woodblocks are reproduced with crisp, sharp lines that even in the most intricately cross-hatched of pieces never descend into a single blurred line. This only highlights the inherent wisdom of the decision to bind the English translations on half-pages alongside the original German text so both may be enjoyed simultaneously.

In closing, I consider *Der Orchideengarten* both a valuable document in the history of weird fiction and also a testament to the care and dedication with which Zagava approaches their craft. In my discussions with Jonas from Zagava, he has stated they are working to restore further issues of *Der Orchideengarten*. Difficulties currently include finding translators who specialize in the genre and tracking down the heirs to secure the rights for publication. Even with such hurdles in place, Jonas assures me Zagava hopes to release the second edition of *Der Orchideengarten* by late summer of 2018 alongside "faux stamps" and framed prints of the best covers from *Der Orchideengarten*'s print run. I myself eagerly await these developments and wish every success to everyone involved.

Tested Patience

June Pulliam

DUANE PESICE, ed. *Test Patterns: Volume 1.* Vacaville, CA: Planet X Publications, 2017. 240 pp. $14.99 tpb. ISBN: 978-0-692-99998-1.

I am a huge fan of the sort of weird television that was pioneered by *The Twilight Zone:* the pared-down stories of how everyday life could take an unnatural twist are still relevant today, thanks in part to the script writing of Rod Serling, Ray Bradbury, Richard Matheson, and Charles Beaumont, among others. And so I was excited about Duane Pesice's anthology *Test Patterns,* which is described on its cover as an "outré collection of short speculative fictions written with classic Television SF/F anthology programming in mind." Sadly, *Test Patterns* does not fulfill the promise made on its cover about containing "tales told in unique ways, employing provocative twists and revelations." Instead, this collection contains too many tales that lack the salient details of a good short story, such as a compelling denouement, or in some instances, even a plot.

The best in the collection include William Tea's "I Am Become Death" and Sarah Walker's "The Snake Beneath the Skin." Tea's story had an original take on the concept of haunting: a military photographer is haunted by the negative images left behind by some of the people incinerated in the nuclear bombing of Hiroshima and Nagasaki after he takes pictures of the blasts' aftermath. Tea gets bonus points for clever character names—Sgt. Rodman, the haunted photographer, is clearly a nod to *Twilight Zone* creator Rod Serling (whose full given name was Rodman), while Dr. Beaumont and Lt. Matheson acknowledge the show's regular writers, Charles Beaumont and Richard Matheson. But the story itself relies so heavily on the interpretation of photographs that are the medium of Rodman's haunting that the story would have been better related in a visual medium. It's just too difficult to visualize the details of these photos, which Rodman believes are sufficiently uncanny to provoke a supernatural encounter.

Sarah Walker's "The Snake Beneath the Skin" is a memorable take on stories about gringos whose sense of cultural superiority is their downfall, as it gives them a false sense of security when they exploit the people of the supposedly conquered culture. This special kind of hubris is revealed to the white protagonist by an acolyte of the Serpent God:

> There are things going on under what you see here. There are layers within layers, even realities within this one. We Mexicanos here know this, and we accept this. You Americans, you fight it, and that's why you are so miserable. That is why you do the drugs. That is why you come to Mexico to party and have sex. You simply refuse to see.

And so, the gringo protagonist finds himself trapped in one of those layers of reality whose existence he could not acknowledge. Walker's deft juxtaposition of the realities of the colonizer and the colonized make this story effective in communicating the peculiar horror of the weird tale.

S. L. Edwards's "Golden Girl," about a puppetmaster's horrifying secret to making life-size puppets, is also notable. This story is a combination of the film *Dead Silence* (2007) and E. T. A. Hoffmann's story "The Sandman" (1816). The puppets' uncannily lifelike qualities were similar to those of the doll Olimpia in Hoffman's story.

Other works in this anthology lack important basic elements of story or are merely weird for the sake of being weird. Phillip Fracassi's "The Judge" tries to be so faithful to everyday reality that it lacks a story arc. One moment a man called to jury duty is flirting with a woman he just met, and the next minute a bomb goes off in the courtroom. The end. Even realistic fiction is expected to have dramatic tension and a climactic arc that is connected to it. Brian O'Connell's "Scenes from a Forgotten Diorama" is more disappointing than "The Judge" because its descriptions of the aforementioned diorama are fascinating in their detail. In 2013, photographs of the diorama were found in the attic of an old house by its new owner. The author tells us at the end that a search of the records of the house itself "proved most fascinating, and more than a little disturbing, when viewed in context with (the photographs of) the diorama to our source, the house was once occupied by [. . . more. . .]" and that's it. This is not a cliffhanger ending; it is just an unfinished story.

Other stories rely so heavily upon well-worn tropes from these old anthology television series that they are predictable and unoriginal. In the dystopia of Peter J. Carter's "Work Group," people are severely punished when they fail to adhere to societal norms, as generally happens in every dystopia ever devised. In this world, robots have taken over most manual labor, such as chicken farming. Humans are now occupied with more important things, such as using toner to maintain the same skin tone as everyone else and guarding one's speech to the degree that it is illegal to express an opposing political view within 30 feet of someone else. And humans are severely punished when they fail to conform in thought and appearance to societal norms or to express belief in a divine creator. Dissidents such as the protagonist are sentenced to re-education camps. Sound familiar, rather like nearly every dystopian work from *1984* to *The Giver* to the Divergent series? Peter Rawlik's "The Nomenclature of Unnamable Things" similarly treads well-worn literary ground: a woman who may or may not be a mental patient works on her version of the *Necronomicon*, which includes names for monsters originally coined by Lovecraft, and her keepers are beginning to lose their ability to deny the reality of what she names her tome. Bill Hand's "You Can't Go Wrong with Grass Fed Beef" is also too predictable in that it relies heavily on established weird television tropes without bothering to expand those ideas. The title alludes to the advice that a butcher gives his customers by way of selling his wares. Of course, the butcher is misrepresenting the cuts of meat in his shop to his customers, who nevertheless find his "grass-fed beef" delicious.

Weird fiction as embodied by anthology television shows like *The Twilight Zone* and later *Alfred Hitchcock Presents, Night Gallery*, and, most recently, *Black Mirror* is akin to magical realism in that the horror presented in it is such a gradual expansion of our reality that its presence is not an aberration that must promptly be shunned by the mind in order to preserve the status quo. Sadly, the majority of the stories in this anthology did not live up to the editor's promise on the book jacket, let alone capture the distorted realities that have made so many of the weird anthology television shows so prescient.

The Banality of Our Bureaucracies

Javier A. Martinez

BENTLEY LITTLE. *The Handyman*. Forest Hill, MD: Cemetery Dance Publications, 2017, 380 pp. $25.00 hc. ISBN: 978-1-58767-616-1.

Bentley Little has been a prolific writer since publishing his first short story, "Witch Woman," in 1985 and his first novel, the Bram Stoker Award–winning *The Revelation,* in 1990. With twenty-vie novels and more than 100 short stories in print, Little has established himself as a serious voice in genre horror. In many ways, he represents the very embodiment of the working writer: consistent, dependable, recognizable, readable. There is no other genre writer who manages to fuse so well the anxiety created by dealing with institutions or their representatives with a supernaturalism that threatens to undermine completely whatever semblance of control his characters attempt to exert over their lives. As with so much horror, Little's protagonists are always victimized by some greater force, some threatening Other. What makes his best work so distinctive, however, is the medium through which this menace manifests itself: an insurance policy, a chain store, a mailman, a charter school, a resort, a university, a house, a handyman. In Little's universe, the most mundane of institutions and personalities foment a state of existential dread revealing a malignancy that threatens the very center of things.

The Handyman tells the story of Daniel Martin, a real estate agent who, quite by chance, discovers that he and his family were not the only victims of a handyman's shoddy work that led to his little brother's death years earlier. Daniel's backstory and his gradual detection of the titular handyman, Frank, make up most of part one of the novel. Part two is an interlude of sorts and is discussed below, and part three continues Daniel and Frank's story, crystalizing the plot lines established in part one and tracing them to the story's final conflict and denouement. Frank is revealed as a malefic character whose influence has affected dozens of hapless homeowners throughout the United States over the course of decades. Daniel's hunt is at once a story of revenge and absolution: he seeks vengeance for his lost brother and his broken family, even as he comes to understand that he and his family were victims, through no fault of their own, of Frank's occult cruelty. The gradual presentation of scenes from Frank's past, Daniel's interaction with those whose lives Frank has destroyed, and Daniel's confrontation with the weight of his personal trauma, not to mention Frank, are effectively presented in an engaging and enjoyable read.

The Handyman is one of Little's better novels. His writing lacks the elegance of some of his contemporaries—Little is not a writer of literary horror like Christopher Buehlman or Brian Evenson—but here the excesses of genre prose are largely absent, as is the penchant for overusing short, declarative, stand-alone phrases that so many genre writers use as a rhetorical shortcut to achieve dread—the literary equivalent of the cinematic cheap shock. Instead, Little's largely first-person narrative is presented in a sober, controlled voice that gradually and consistently (at least within the logic of the story) builds toward the story's revelation and climax.

Little's greatest challenge has always been the pacing of his conclusions and denouements. Some of those problems persist here, but in a mostly muted way. What is especially of interest is Little's narrative decision to break up the story into three parts. One could skip the second part altogether and not lose the details of the story. In fact, one could argue that the narrative drive of the story would benefit from deleting the second part and combining parts one and three into one seamless, and shorter, novel. But the power of the second part is key to the effectiveness of *The Handyman*: it deepens the work, presenting Frank's ever-spreading network of corruption across the national landscape. The various viewpoints—an angst-ridden teen in 1979 Los Angeles; an interracial lesbian couple in Oregon in 2010; a hardware store manager in Seattle in 1995; a construction worker and charged sex offender in Denver in 1988; a home inspector in Amarillo in 1999; an alienated veteran from the war in Afghanistan in Austin in 2003; and four story extracts from newspapers in Arizona, Fresno, Salt Lake City, and Albuquerque—all show the devastating and wide-reaching effects of the handyman's atrocities, further characterizing him as a malevolent force masquerading as an inexpert jack-of-all-trades and cementing Little's uniquely American brand of horror.

The concluding section of the second part gives insight into Frank's origin, describing his time in Vietnam in 1966 and the terrible knowledge he gained there. The idea of importing dangerous or forbidden knowledge from the East is an old and overused cliché that is especially problematic in today's environment, when even the most casual of readers understands that the use of blanket racial concepts often leads to racist subtexts if not outright racist characterizations. But Little is able to walk a fine line here: yes, he uses a tired generic trope, but the evil has already been ostracized and condemned as such in its homeland. It is only in the hands of the imperialist that it becomes recharged and deployed in the Western world. And, without giving too much away, it is accurate to say that the evil that Frank embraces and imports seems more than content to stay where it is.

Little is especially hard on American institutions and culture in general, and there is a reactionary frustration that fuels his work. As he states in an interview from 2012:

> The ideas for most of my novels come from personal experience. As a writer, I've always been absurdly dependent on the mail, and while working for a small town weekly newspaper, I had a bizarre encounter with a postal worker. So I came up with the idea for *The Mailman*. . . . In that same Arizona town, I saw a huge chain store put a lot of local shopkeepers out of business and came up with *The Store*. Problems with insurance companies inspired *The Policy*. Problems with a homeowner's association inspired *The Association*. My own letter-writing proclivities gave me the idea for *Dispatch*. . . . So, really, most of my work involves situations in my own life that I deal with metaphorically and reflect through the lens of horror fiction.[1]

Little's fiction is so compelling because it acutely amplifies the crushing banality of our bureaucracies, and our never-ending frustrations with its concomitant bureaucrats. This undercurrent

---

1. http://www.thehorrorzine.com/Special/BentleyLittle/BentleyLittle.html

of anger informs all Little's fiction. One can read his work as a type of resistance to, if not outright rejection of, the systems of modern American society. Put another way, his characters would most likely have voted for Trump in 2016. This is not meant as a criticism or an insult, as many folks in literary studies would probably take it. Rather, it is an observation of Little's characters, who are often white males under fifty who find themselves frustrated and confused by a landscape that is changing in ways that chafe their frames of reference and which they consequently find threatening. Nevertheless, there is a humanism in Little's fiction that always rises to the surface. His characters want normal lives, steady jobs, a home, a safe place to share with those they love. They are genuinely relatable every-persons who find themselves in situations they are psychologically and emotionally unprepared to deal with, yet do so all the same. Little's most successful novels manage to sustain these sometimes conflicting values and impulses, a balancing act he performs quite well in *The Handyman*.

A Dark, Intense, Fantastic Debut

Greg Gbur

NADIA BULKIN. *She Said Destroy: Stories*. Petaluma, CA: Word Horde, 2017. 264 pp. $16.99 tpb. ISBN: 978-1-939905-33-8.

"At the beginning, at the very very beginning of time, the General ate a bullet."

So begins "Intertropical Convergence Zone," the first story in Nadia Bulkin's debut collection of weird fiction, *She Said Destroy*. This opening is a perfect encapsulation of the stories of the volume as a whole: surprising, compelling, and unflinching in their depiction of violence against, and between, human beings.

She Said Destroy contains thirteen stories taken from Bulkin's entire publication history to date. The earliest, "Intertropical Convergence Zone," first appeared in 2008, and the most recent, "No Gods, No Masters," appears for the first time in this book. The accolades that many of the tales have already accrued make their quality inarguable: "Only Unity Saves the Damned," for instance, was reprinted in the *Year's Best Dark Fantasy and Horror: 2015*, and "Violet is the Color of Your Energy" was reprinted in *Year's Best Weird Fiction* (2016).

The dark intensity of the tales is impressive. Bulkin was living in Indonesia in 1998 during an intense year-long period of civil unrest and violence known as the Reformasi, which resulted in the forced resignation of President Suharto after a thirty-year reign. This inspired Bulkin to study political science, and she received her M.A. in international politics in 2009. Her background, and her education, inform several of the stories of *She Said Destroy,* which feature what Bulkin herself calls "sociopolitical horror," a blend of Southeast Asian politics and supernatural horror. Bulkin's perspective is a truly unique one in horror and makes for compelling reading.

While I was reading the collection, I was struck by how *broken* most of the characters are, as human beings. There is a lieutenant who has convinced himself that any sacrifice is worth a political cause; a family that is unable to let go of a lost loved one; a group of teens who are willing to do anything to escape their small-town fate; a young woman who is desperate for companionship, though she is in an area arguably infested with humanity; a cleaning woman who will live a lie in order to gain attention; and a man who is haunted by the knowledge of his family history, among others. The weaknesses and pain of these characters lead them inexorably to their fates. To me, an overall theme of the stories is that our horror is born of the damage that has been done to us.

A summary of a few of the stories will give an impression of the overall themes and tone of the book.

In "Intertropical Convergence Zone," the General seeks power from a local sorcerer to support his political campaign. But each ingredient requested by the sorcerer is more difficult to acquire than the last, and eventually the benefit may not be worth the cost.

When a monster kills a group of teens on a remote farm in "And When She Was Bad," the sole survivor must face the creature, and her own demons, on her own.

A trio of teenagers capture a viral video of an encounter with a witch in "Only Unity Saves the Damned," but their newfound fame draws the attention and scrutiny not only of the local community, but of things that should have best been left alone.

In "Seven Minutes in Heaven," a young woman becomes obsessed with a neighboring town that was completely exterminated in an industrial accident and finds that she has more of a kinship with those lost residents than she could ever have imagined.

Revenge and love are dueling obsessions in "Girl, I Love You," set in a world where magical attacks—and deadly curses—are achievable for almost anyone. But when one cruel girl turns out to be immune to such threats, the balance of power is shifted—and a mission is passed on.

The fortunes of Abigail and Nate seem to change abruptly with the apparent crash of a meteorite on their farm one night in "Violet Is the Color of Your Energy." But the new crops that grow seem . . . not right, and Nate's obsession with them threatens to tear their lives apart.

In "Truth Is Order and Order Is Truth," an exiled princess

leads her followers on a dangerous trip to her ancestral home—and finds that she has a heritage that transcends human limitations and human desires.

The failings of a cursed family in "No Gods, No Masters" leads them toward utter destruction, not only for themselves and their loved ones but for all humanity.

As one can deduce from the descriptions, several of the stories draw upon the Cthulhu Mythos. "Violet Is the Color of Your Energy" takes Lovecraft's "The Colour out of Space" and gives it a disturbing flavor of domestic abuse and horror. "Truth Is Order and Order Is Truth" takes Lovecraft's famed fictional city of Innsmouth and transports its monstrous inhabitants to a rural Indonesian setting. Both tales are much more human—that is, filled with actual believable people—than Lovecraft's originals.

As can also be seen from the earlier descriptions, Bulkin does not limit herself to the world as we know it, and several of the tales are set in realities with fundamental differences from our own. Bulkin has great fun in exploring the implications of these differences, from the world of curses in "Girl, I Love You" to a world in which the dead refuse to move on to their rest in "The Five Stages of Grief." In "Pugelbone," she introduces a science fiction setting where humans are so tightly packed into cities that new horrible forms of life are able to thrive.

The book includes an excellent introduction by Paul Tremblay, which provides more details about Bulkin's literary and personal history, giving further context for the stories one is about to read.

From the variety of settings, and characters, and styles, it is difficult to predict what to expect from tale to tale in *She Said Destroy*. It is an impressive volume and a fantastic debut collection from Nadia Bulkin.

About the Contributors

Michael J. Abolafia is an editor, writer, and archivist with a B.A. in English from Columbia University, and co-editor of *Dead Reckonings*.

Jason V Brock is a writer, editor, filmmaker, composer, artist, scholar, and speaker. He has been widely published online, in comic books, magazines, and anthologies.

Ramsey Campbell is an English horror fiction writer, editor, and critic who has been writing for well over fifty years. He is frequently cited as one of the leading writers in the field. His website is www.ramseycampbell.com.

Scott Connors is a leading expert on Clark Ashton Smith.

Sam Cowan is the founder of Dim Shores, a publisher that presents short-run high-quality fiction from the horizons of the Weird Renaissance and beyond. See dimshores.storenvy.com.

Ryne Davis is a weird fiction enthusiast and collector from Walnut, Illinois.

Nicholas Diak is an academic focusing primarily on Italian Eurospy films, neo-peplum films, and post-industrial music. He is also the co-creator and co-chair of the Ann Radcliffe Academic Conference held in conjunction with StokerCon.

Dave Felton's scratchboard illustrations have appeared in books published by Dim Shores, Dunhams Manor Press, and the *Lovecraft eZine*.

Greg Gbur is a professor of physics and optical science at UNCC Charlotte. For more than a decade he has written a blog called "Skulls in the Stars" (skullsinthestars.com) about physics, horror fiction, and curious intersections between them. He has written a number of introductions to classic reprinted horror novels for Valancourt Books.

Acep Hale is a magician, comedian, and writer who currently resides in Brooklyn, NY.

Alex Houstoun is a co-editor of *Dead Reckonings*.

S. T. Joshi is the author of such critical studies as *The Weird Tale* (1990), *H. P. Lovecraft: The Decline of the West* (1990), and *Unutterable Horror: A History of Supernatural Fiction* (2012). He has prepared corrected editions of H. P. Lovecraft's work for Arkham House and annotated editions of the weird tales of Lovecraft, Algernon Blackwood, Lord Dunsany, M. R. James, Arthur Machen, and Clark Ashton Smith for Penguin Classics, as well as the anthology *American Supernatural Tales* (2007).

Randall Larson has been publishing fiction and nonfiction since the 1970s, ranging from several books about Robert Bloch, essays on Joseph Payne Brennan, weird poetry in *Spectral Realms,* a number of Lovecraftian stories and essays, and articles and CD liner notes about film music.

Javier A. Martinez was managing editor of *Extrapolation* for fifteen years. A former department chair, college dean, and university provost, he is currently Professor of English in the Department of Literatures & Cultural Studies at the University of Texas Rio Grande Valley.

Daniel Pietersen is a writer of weird fiction and horror philosophy. He has a blog of fragmentary work and other thoughts at https://constantuniversity.wordpress.com.

June Pulliam teaches courses on horror fiction at Louisiana State University. She is the author of *Monstrous Bodies: Feminine Power in Young Adult Horror Fiction,* as well as many articles on fantastic young adult fiction, Roald Dahl, and zombie studies.

Géza A. G. Reilly is a writer and critic with an interest in twentieth-century American genre literature. A Canadian expatriate, he now lives in the wilds of Florida with his wife, Andrea, and their cat, Mim.

Jim Rockhill is the editor of volumes collecting fiction by E. T.

A. Hoffmann, Joseph Sheridan Le Fanu, and Bob Leman; and co-editor of Jane Rice's collected fiction, the essay collection *Reflections in a Glass Darkly,* and the anthology *Dreams of Shadow and Smoke.* He has contributed introductions, essays and reviews for books by Seabury Quinn and Brian Showers, *Supernatural Literature of the World, Horror Literature through History, Encyclopedia of the Vampire, The Freedom of Fantastic Things, Warnings to the Curious, Lost Souls,* and *The Green Book,* as well as a variety of other encyclopedias and journals.

Christopher Ropes is an author and musician who lives in New Jersey with his partner, their two children, and their cats. His work has been published by Dunhams Manor/Dynatox Industries and in the first issue of *Vastarien: A Literary Journal.*

Darrell Schweitzer is an American writer, editor, and critic in the field of speculative fiction. Much of his focus has been on dark fantasy and horror, although he also does work in science fiction and fantasy. His latest book *is The Threshold of Forever: Essays and Reviews.*

Farah Rose Smith is a writer, weird artist, and the publisher of *Mantid.* More information about her work can be found at www.facebook.com/farahrosesmith and about *Mantid* at www.facebook.com/mantidmagazine.

Bev Vincent is the author of several books, most recently *The Dark Tower Companion.* His work has been nominated for the Bram Stoker Award (twice), the Edgar Award, and the ITW Thriller Award, and he won the 2010 Al Blanchard Award. His reviews also appear at *Onyx Reviews* (onyxreviews.com). He is a contributing editor with *Cemetery Dance* and has published more than eighty short stories. His web presence is bevvincent.com.

Hank Wagner is a respected critic and journalist. Among the many publications in which his work regularly appears are *Cemetery Dance* and *Mystery Scene.*